RICKY CLEMONS

PUBLISHED BY FIEDLI PUBLISHING, INC.

Copyright ©2019, Ricky Clemons
ALL RIGHTS RESERVED.

No part of this publication may be reproduced, stored in a retrieval system, or transmitted in any form or by any means—electronic, mechanical, photo-copy, recording, or any other—except for brief quotation in reviews, without the prior permission of the author or publisher.

ISBN: 978-1-948638-47-0

Published by

Fideli Publishing, Inc.
119 W. Morgan St.
Martinsville, IN 46151
www.FideliPublishing.com

Table of Contents

Red Roses of Our Faith 1
I Had to Choose 2
Having Faith in Jesus 4
The Old and the New Testament 5
Standing Up for the Sabbath 6
Jesus Can 7
Jesus was Human 8
The Mountain 9
Will Step All Over Our Toes 10
Does Everybody
Get a Second Chance? 11
Attracted 12
We Didn't Choose this Life 13
Influence 14
God is the Beginning and the End 15
Behind a Mask 16
Life Can Tie Us Up in Knots 17
Will Not Forget Your Past Sins 18
Will Be Shocked 19
One Day at a Time to Be Saved 20
Mental Powers 21
The Church Pews 22
A Smile and Kind Words 23

Pride Spoke to Me 24
Conspiracy 25
Racism is Nothing New Today... 26
To the Edge 27
Alliance 28
Walk on Water Faith.. 29
We Can't Solve All of Our Choices.. 30
Down in the Ocean of the Heart 31
Shipwrecked 32
Plant His Garden 33
Around the Clock Faith... 34
Jesus Knows My Heart... 35
Many of the
Worst Kinds of Criminals 36
God Created Eve for Adam 38
And That's Just the Way It Is... 39
Can Take Away 40
May Never See Again... 41
Would You Want to Become a Christian? 42
Caused by Sin 43
What Jesus Wants 44
We Can Want to Rush the Lord 45
Want to be Worshiped... 46
Some People Believe 47
You Can't Judge Someone.. 48

Who Don't Believe	49
We Can't	50
We Can Have No Idea	51
Spiritual Exercise	52
We Are Not Without Sin	53
You Will Know	54
What Matters to Jesus	55
Love to Receive	56
Many People Don't Care	57
Fit Into	58
Will Not Accept the Truth	59
A Mystery	60
The Lord Can Use Anyone	61
The Lord is Always on Time	62
My Body is Your Holy Temple	63
The Church Will Still Go On	64
A Lot of People	65
Children	66
We Have to Ask	67
Missing Out	68
For All Who are Still Alive	69
Your Enemy	70
Perfection	71
We Christians Need To	72
It's Not Our Time to Judge	73

Our Little Hardships 74
If We Love the Lord Jesus Christ 76
The Same Temptations 77
May Not Know Why 78
Are Too Comfortable 79
Dangerous Waters of Life 80
What is Real 81
Talking Too Much 82
Jesus is Always Fair 83
Will You Still? 84
Deep 85
The Splendor of God's Love 86
It's Not Me It's You, O Lord 87
You Looked Down Through 88
More and More 89
What Can Be Better? 90
There is No Better Truth 91
We Can Take Time for Granted 92
Heroic 93
God Has a Purpose for Us 94
There is a Lot More to Life 95
Will Go On and On 96
It's Nothing Wrong 97
We are All Guilty 98
Will Pretty Much 99

Christian	100
I Am Like	101
O Lord, I Need You This Day	102
It Doesn't Matter	103
Trials	104
Even if We Only	105
When You Answer My Prayers	106
O Lord, You Will Surely	107
It's a Foolish Thing	108
When We Pray	109
That is Hard Reality	110
Grow on You and Me	111
Heart Is In	112
Boast About Jesus Christ	113
Is a Prison to be Locked Up In	114
So Amazing	115
To Become a Citizen of Heaven	116
Very Often Cautious	117
God is All	118
Jesus Was a Sinless Man of Action	120
Can Be Told	121
A Candle's Light to Shine	122
Sooner or Later	123
The Mind	124
Looking Down on Us	125

There Are People Who	126
We All Have	127
A Spiritual Warming	128
The Spiritual Family	129
God Chooses All	130
The Greatest Experience	131
What is This World Coming To?	132
Life Can	133
Commercials	134
Human Beings are Human Beings	135
I Am Going to Make It	136
First Impressions	137
The Door on Our Hearts	138
The Spiritual Ground	139
The Hard Way	140
Will We Pass God's Test?	141
A Story to Tell	142
Reach	143
We Shouldn't Complain	144
Other Worlds	145
Spiritually Insane	146
This World Can't Put an End To	147
My Life is a Lot Better	148
We May Feel Like	149
Highway	150

Red Roses of Our Faith

The red rose of our faith in Jesus Christ gives us a beautiful, renewed life in Jesus.

Red roses are beautiful.

My faith in Jesus and your faith in Jesus Christ is a beautiful faith for the world to see.

My red roses of faith and your red roses of faith are very well seen in our spiritual gifts in the church.

Beautiful red roses are so captivating to look at.

Our red roses of faith in Jesus can be so captivating to many people who love to look at our faith in our actions about Jesus.

A beautiful red rose can cause someone to feel good.

A beautiful red rose can brighten up someone's life.

A beautiful red rose can put a smile on someone's face.

Our beautiful red roses of faith will cause Jesus to smile upon our lives.

Red roses are very eye-catching.

Our red roses of faith in Jesus is very eye-catching to the angels in heaven.

Red roses will cause many women to cheer up after feeling their birth pains from having a baby.

We can always be cheered up, even on our bad days, by our red roses of faith in Jesus.

That faith is very beautiful beyond our birth pains of life.

I Had to Choose

I had to choose to love drugs or love Jesus.

When I was in the Army, I was a combat engineer.

I became a SP4 in rank in one year and made soldier of the month for my company.

But then, I started using drugs and became hooked on them.

I loved drugs so much that I was using every day.

Eventually the drugs made me sick and I had to be discharged with a medical honorable discharge.

I had received some medical treatment in the hospital, where I was treated for a few months.

I had to come back home to live with my mother, step-father and two sisters.

They welcomed me back home.

They would go to church every Saturday morning and come back home in the afternoon.

I decided to go to church with them.

I liked going to church and I was baptized some months later.

I met a young woman who was not in the church.

We got involved with each other and I left my parent's house to live with her.

We began to have some problems while we both were using drugs.

The problems got so bad that I tried to take my own life by taking sleeping pills.

My girlfriend saved my life and I woke up in the hospital the next day.

I decided to go back home to live with my parents, who readily accepted me back home

I went back to church with them.

I began to grow much stronger in my Lord Jesus.

I made up my mind to love and obey Him and not to love the drugs anymore.

I chose to love Jesus, who set me free from the drugs.

Jesus gave me a second chance to choose to love Him.

Jesus had used my girlfriend to save my life so I could live to see the day when I would choose to love Him.

Having Faith in Jesus

Can anyone do works in Jesus' name and have no faith in Jesus Christ?

Would those works please Jesus?

Anyone in the church can do some good things and not truly give Jesus the glory and the praise.

Anyone in the church can use their spiritual gifts and not truly love Jesus.

Can we hold leadership positions in the church and not truly believe in Jesus?

Can we pray to Jesus and not truly worship Him?

Having faith in Jesus is believing that He exists, even though we don't see him.

The Pharisees were religious, but they didn't believe in Jesus.

The Pharisees prayed, but they didn't believe in Jesus.

The Pharisees knew the law, but they didn't believe in Jesus.

The only way to please Jesus is by faith.

Having faith in Jesus is having a pure heart with Him.

Having faith in Jesus is being made right in God's eyesight by the righteousness of Jesus.

We are not being made right in God's eyesight by our work, which can look right when our hearts may be sinful.

The Old and the New Testament

The animal sacrifices in the Old Testament were pointing to God's son, Jesus Christ, who would be the lamb of God.

Jesus had sacrificed His life on the cross for the sins of the world.

Every time someone would sin against God, he or she would have to sacrifice an animal for God to forgive them of their sins.

The Old Testament talked about a messiah who would come to this world to save people from their sins.

Prophets of old talked about the root of David, who is Jesus Christ.

Prophets of old talked about a messiah.

All the animal sacrifices led to Jesus Christ, who would sacrifice His life for the sins of the world.

Because Jesus gave up His life for our sins, we need no more animal sacrifices.

We can't separate the New Testament from the Old Testament.

If we sin against God, we can go to Jesus and ask Him to forgive us.

We don't have to go and buy a lamb and kill it to ask God to forgive us of our sins.

Jesus Christ was our ultimate sacrifice for our sins.

The Old Testament points us to Jesus Christ, who was born into this world in the New Testament.

Jesus lived up in heaven in the Old Testament.

Jesus came to this world in the New Testament.

Standing Up for the Sabbath

I dreamed about standing up for the Sabbath.

I dreamed that I and my deceased mother were in a place that looked like a small town.

My mother and I walked into a church where we heard some music sounding so divine.

When we entered the church, we saw a woman playing a piano, and another woman was sitting down in the pew.

Yet another woman said out loud, "This man has something to tell you both and it's about keeping the Sabbath day holy." The woman also said, "He's not a preacher."

I said, "I'm a poet and songwriter."

The scene changed and my mother and I were walking together, while she was talking to me.

We walked up to a building that looked like a center where people would go to have activities.

We entered the center and saw some people sitting down.

There was a woman who said with a loud voice, "You all need to listen and hear about the Sabbath."

My mother wanted to sit down, so I pulled out a chair that was between two people.

My mother sat down in the chair and rested.

Then all of a sudden, some police officers rushed into the center and pulled me outside, where they arrested me for standing up for the Sabbath.

I woke up out of my dream and realized that this was a sign of the things that will one day happen to Sabbath day keepers.

Jesus Can

If we are sick, Jesus can help us to get well when the doctor is not around to help us get well.

Jesus can help us to understand His holy word, when the Sabbath school teacher may not be able to help us understand.

Jesus can give us the strength to live right, when sermons from the preacher may not be so uplifting.

Jesus can comfort our minds when things go wrong in our lives.

Jesus can be there for us when no one knows if we are alive.

Jesus can do anything for us to know that it's Him who won't leave us alone to be by ourselves when we need him.

Jesus was Human

God gave us His ten commandments to keep because He knows that we are human and will be tempted by the devil to sin against Him.

Being human is no excuse to willfully sin against the Lord. We know right from wrong.

The Lord will not allow us to be tempted in ways that make us believe that He can't help us to resist the devil's temptations.

Even though we are human, the Lord can give us strength to resist temptations.

God's commandments will let us know that God can help us humans to live right, beyond our human behavior.

We all are human, and can thank Jesus for being human too, and helping us to overcome our sins.

Jesus was tempted like us humans, but he did not sin against God.

Jesus was tempted in many ways that you and I will not be tempted in.

Jesus was so much more human than you and me.

Many people will say, "I am only human," and make Jesus look worthless.

When Jesus was human, he overcame our sins and gave us the right to live beyond our human habits that can degrade us.

The Mountain

There was a man who had prepared himself to climb up the mountain to see God.

He had all of his mountain gear to make the climb.

One day in the early morning he began to climb up the mountain.

He saw another man having some problems and doubting he'd make the climb.

The man asked for help with his climb.

The first man laughed and said, "You are on your own. This is your climb."

So, the man who was prepared kept on climbing up the mountain until he reached the top, but God wasn't there to meet him.

The man didn't understand why God wasn't there at the top.

So, he climbed back down the mountain, where he saw the other man still having problems and needing help.

The other man asked him, "Did you see God at the top of the mountain?"

He said, "No, I didn't see God."

The next day, God spoke to the man and said, "I didn't meet you at the top of the mountain because you only cared about yourself and didn't help the other man with his climb up the mountain, even though he was climbing with the same purpose as you."

God also said, "You are your brother's keeper and should always help him make his climb to meet me."

The moral of the story is: God loves to meet a selfless heart.

Will Step All Over Our Toes

The Holy Spirit will step all over our toes with the truth, if our hearts are not right with the Lord.

If our hearts are not right with the Lord, our hearts will not be right with one another.

The Holy Spirit will step all over our toes with the truth, if our hearts are not right with one another.

The truth is for us all to live by.

The truth shows no respect of persons.

Some church folks believe that they are smarter than the Holy Spirit.

They believe that the Holy Spirit can't see what they are doing wrong.

They believe that the Holy Spirit will let them get away with the wrong things they say.

The Holy Spirit will step all over our toes with the truth of God's holy word.

The Holy Spirit is all about the truth of Jesus Christ.

Our hearts are not always true to Jesus, who loves everybody and can save us all from being lost in sin.

If we have the Holy Spirit in us, we will feel guilty for doing something wrong.

The Holy Spirit will step all over our toes with the truth.

The Holy Spirit is not picky with the truth for us.

Some church folks are picky about what they believe to be true or not true to them.

Does Everybody Get a Second Chance?

Does everybody get a second chance to confess and repent of their sins and believe in Jesus Christ?

We know that a lot of babies die.

They are not at a mature age to know right from wrong.

We know that many young children die.

They didn't know right from wrong.

God is always fair to seal them to go to heaven when Jesus comes back again.

The bible says for children to obey their parents.

If they don't obey, their lives will be cut short.

Will disobedient children make it to heaven?

Does God give them a second chance to obey their parents?

We know that God is fair with everybody.

If a child is old enough to know right from wrong, will he or she be held accountable for their sins?

Many little children do foolish things that cause them to lose their lives.

Does God give them a second chance to not do something foolish that could cause them to lose their lives?

We do worship a second chance God who knows even the minds and hearts of children.

God gives disobedient children a second chance to obey their parents or anyone who tells them to not do this or that.

Many obedient children die young.

They will make it to heaven.

Attracted

A married man can be attracted to other women, but he must be faithful to his wife.

A married woman can be attracted to other men, but she must be faithful to her husband.

Just because a man is attracted to a woman doesn't mean that he has to marry her.

Just because a woman is attracted to a man doesn't mean she has to marry him.

Just because a man is attracted to a woman doesn't mean he must have sex with her.

Just because a woman is attracted to a man doesn't mean that she must have sex with him.

You can be attracted to someone and go your separate ways.

You can be attracted to someone and just be friends.

Just because you are attracted to someone doesn't mean that he or she is right for you.

Jesus Christ, our Lord and savior, was a sinless man, but that doesn't mean he wasn't attracted to women.

I believe that many women were attracted to Jesus.

Was Jesus tempted to get married?

We don't know that.

Jesus was the son of God.

He created women.

Jesus was all about saving women from their sins, as well as saving men.

We Didn't Choose this Life

We didn't choose this life that we were born into.

We didn't choose this life that will give us some good days and some bad days.

We didn't choose this life that can abuse us spiritually, emotionally, mentally and physically.

We didn't choose this life that can give us unpredicted situations.

We didn't choose this life that we were born into.

When we were born into this life, we didn't know how life would treat us.

When we were born into this life, we didn't know what we would experience.

When we were born into this life, we didn't know what we would go through.

We didn't choose this life when Jesus Christ, our Lord, chose us to be born and live in this life.

Jesus chose us to exist in this life.

Jesus chose us to choose to love and obey Him or not love and obey Him in this life that we didn't choose to be born in.

Influence

What we say will have some influence on one another.

What we believe will have some influence on one another.

How we dress will have some influence on one another.

Our opinions will have some influence on one another.

Our achievements will have some influence on one another.

Our failures will have some influence on one another.

What we do will have some influence on one another.

Our victories will have some influence on one another.

How we live our lives will have some influence on one another.

If we are good, we will have some influence on ourselves and others.

If we are evil, we will have some influence on ourselves and others.

Jesus Christ lived on this earth without sin.

The Pharisees believed that Jesus was a bad influence on them, when it was actually them who were a bad influence on Jesus.

Jesus is the best influence for all the world to believe in Him and be saved.

God is the Beginning and the End

God is the beginning and the end.

Nothing existed before God.

God existed before He ever created heaven and earth.

God is the beginning, and no one knows how God began.

God is the beginning, and no one knows how long God has been around.

God is the beginning and the end.

We don't know God's beginning and we don't know God's end.

It's like not knowing the height, depth, and width of billions of galaxies.

Wanting to know the beginning and the end of God is like wanting to walk on the ocean without sinking into it.

God knows why he can't tell us his beginning and end.

We would all die and not exist anymore before God would tell us why he is the beginning and the end.

Lucifer wanted to be the beginning and the end, even though God created him.

Lucifer wanted to be God, but he lost his perfection when he rebelled against God, who is perfect in every word that he says and everything he does.

God is worthy to be the beginning and the end.

Our beginning was in our mother's womb and our end will be in the grave.

God won't let us end there if we are saved in His son, Jesus Christ, who is one with God and the Holy Spirit.

God is the beginning and the end of all existence.

Behind a Mask

Terrorists love to hide behind a mask and not show their faces.

They don't want to be identified by anyone they want to kill.

A thief loves to hide behind a mask so he can't be identified when he robs someone.

The little children love to hide behind masks on Halloween night and get their bags filled with candy.

Some kidnappers love to hide behind a mask so their victims can't see their faces and they can get the ransom.

Can you and I hide behind a spiritual mask that hides our motives so people can't see?

The Lord sees us all for who we truly are.

We can't hide our true self from the Lord.

Whether we are hiding behind a physical mask or a spiritual mask, the Lord will always see the true face of our hearts. They can't hide from him.

We can put our spiritual masks on, but the Lord will take them off with the truth of His holy word.

Life Can Tie Us Up in Knots

We can lose some loved ones and feel so lost in life.

Life can tie us up in knots.

The uncertain can hit us hard and knock us down in sorrow.

Life can tie us up in knots.

Time can't promise to be on our side.

Life can tie us up in knots.

Feelings can get so numb to suppress the pain.

Life can tie us up in knots.

Questions are not always answered.

Life can tie us up in knots.

Protection is not always available for the unexpected.

Life can tie us up in knots.

Jesus can untie us and give us some hope in His mercy.

Jesus can untie us and give us some hope in His grace.

Jesus can untie us and give us some hope in His time to heal our hearts that can get tied up in the knots of brokenness.

Will Not Forget Your Past Sins

Some people will not forget the past.

You and I have moved on beyond the past, but some people will remind us of what we did then.

Some people love to hold onto your past sins, even though you have confessed and repented of them unto the Lord.

They won't forget your past sins, no matter what good things you do in Jesus Christ's name.

If some people can't find any fault in you today, they will go back in the past to find fault in what you did wrong to them or someone else.

My past sins and your past sins are unforgettable to some people who will hold your past sins against you.

If Jesus was that way, we would be better off to have never been born.

If we confess and repent of our sins, Jesus will forgive us and not remember our past sins that we committed against Him.

People who love to dig up past sins are like digging up a grave to find nothing but bones.

Jesus forgave you and me of our past sins, and no one can bring our sins back.

They are gone forever in Jesus' eyes.

Some people will never forget our past sins.

Will Be Shocked

Some people will be shocked to be in the first resurrection.

Some people will be shocked to see some other people in the first resurrection.

The first resurrection is about Jesus Christ raising the righteous dead to take them to heaven when he comes back again.

Many people will be shocked to not see the people who they believed to be saved in Jesus.

Some righteous people will be shocked to see some other people in the first resurrection.

They believed that those people were lost in their sins.

Being raised up in the first resurrection will shock some people who will be surprised to see themselves going to heaven with Jesus.

Being raised up in the second resurrection will shock many people who will be surprised to see themselves going to hell with the devil and his fallen angels.

Jesus will not be shocked about who will go to heaven and who will go to hell.

Jesus knows the whole heart.

One Day at a Time to Be Saved

It will take one day at a time to be saved in Jesus Christ.

Many people believe that once you are saved, you are always saved.

If that was true, then no one would stray away from Jesus.

There are people who were saved in Jesus, but then they turned their backs on Him.

It will take one day at a time to be saved in Jesus Christ.

We have to make our choices one day at a time.

We will choose to love and obey Jesus one day at a time.

Another day has brought some people so much pain.

They let that pain get the best of them, and then turn their backs on Jesus.

They let the pain cause them to give up on Jesus.

We must believe in Jesus one day at a time to be saved.

We can't always be saved in one day.

We can want to stop trusting Jesus, especially if we lose a loved one who we loved so very much.

Job's wife turned her back on God.

She told Job to curse God and die.

She didn't talk like a saved woman on that day when she told Job to curse God and die.

It will take one day at a time to be saved.

Mental Powers

If you use your mental powers to uplift the name of Jesus Christ, He will give your mind more mental powers so your thoughts can produce words of glory and praise unto Him.

God's word will give us mental powers to know the truth.

Praying to the Lord will give you and me mental powers to believe that He will hear and answer our prayers.

Loving and obeying Jesus Christ will give us mental powers so we will know we are saved in Him.

Everybody in this world has some mental powers to think good or bad thoughts.

Everybody has some mental powers to say something good or bad.

If we confess and repent of our sins, Jesus will give us more mental powers so we can turn away from our sins.

We all have mental powers to make choices.

The more we get closer to Jesus, the more mental powers Jesus will give to us to keep our minds on Him.

The Church Pews

The church pews are crying out unto the Lord for more and more people to sit down on them.

The church pews are waiting on people to confess and repent of their sins and be baptized to join the church.

The church pews are watching to see if you and I are real about the Lord.

The church pews have seen people join the church and leave the church.

The church pews know all who are faithful unto the Lord.

The church pews have unaware angels sitting down on them.

The church pews are tired of hypocrites sitting on them.

The church pews are happy to see us worshiping the Lord and giving Him the glory and the praise.

A Smile and Kind Words

One day, on a Wednesday afternoon, I went to the public library.

I went inside the library and walked up to the front desk.

A middle-aged woman and a young woman were standing behind the desk, talking to each other with laughter in their voices.

When the young, attractive woman turned around to face me, I asked her, "Will you make a copy of each of these pages?" and gave them to her.

She made the copies, gave me a big smile and asked, "How are you doing?"

Her big, radiant smile and her kind words lifted me up, and I smiled back at her and asked how she was doing.

When I left the library, I was feeling good because of her smile and the kind words she spoke to me.

Even if some things aren't going so well in your life, we don't have to show it on our faces or say it with our words.

Giving someone a smile and saying some kind words can lift someone up and make their day much better.

We Christians are so blessed to be saved in Jesus Christ.

Because of Jesus, we have something to smile about.

We have something good to talk about, no matter what the bad days that come our way.

I don't know if that young woman is a Christian or not, but her smile and kind words surely lifted me up.

Pride Spoke to Me

One day, in the afternoon, pride spoke to me and said, "I can make you look good before others if you exalt me for saying that I can do this and I did that."

The words of pride swelled me up, making me think highly of myself and making me want to look good.

Pride didn't want me to say that the Lord had blessed me to do this and do that.

Pride spoke to me again and said, "I want you to make me look good in what you say and what you do so that I get the glory and the praise."

Pride spoke to me for the third time and said to me, "Don't humble yourself. I can make you look really good before others who see you not being a fool for exalting yourself in a slick and sly way so they wont' see it."

I looked at pride with the Holy Spirit in my heart letting me know that God hates pride.

I said to pride, "I will make Jesus Christ, my Lord, look good. He is worthy to look good, but you, Mr. Pride, will ruin yourself."

Conspiracy

There are people who will conspire to take away what belongs to someone else.

They will carefully plan out and follow through on it.

There are people who will conspire to ruin someone's good name.

They carefully plan and spread rumors.

There are people who will conspire to kill other people.

They will carefully plan to kill them at just the right time.

There are people who will conspire to harm someone.

They will carefully plan to injure that person.

Some political leaders will conspire against other political leaders.

They will carefully plan to make them look bad.

Conspiracy is nothing new.

Lucifer conspired against God up in heaven.

He planned to take over God's holy throne.

The Pharisees conspired against Jesus Christ.

They tried to Kill Jesus because He was a big threat to them.

Every day there are people who are conspiring against others they don't like.

They carefully plan to give others trouble.

The devil is conspiring against every human being.

He will carefully plan to destroy us all and make us lost.

Jesus has got the victory for us all.

Racism is Nothing New Today

Back in the bible days, many of the Jews were racist.

They didn't like the gentiles.

They believed that all the gentiles were pagans.

Many of the Jews didn't accept the gentiles who became Christians, because they believed in Jesus Christ.

Many of the Jews believed that gentiles had to be circumcised to be saved.

Many of the Jews believed that they were better than the gentiles.

The Jews believed that the gentiles were unclean people.

Racism is nothing new today.

Many people of one race believe they are better than people of another race.

They believe that if their skin complexion is lighter, they are better.

They believe they are smarter than another race of people, as well.

Lucifer became a racist up in heaven.

Lucifer wanted to remove God from His holy throne.

Lucifer wanted to remove God from heaven so he could take control of all the angels.

To the Edge

O Lord, you have sent me to the edge of my mind, so that I will know that it's you who keeps my thoughts sane.

O Lord, you have sent me to the edge of my heart, so I will feel Your favor upon my motives.

O Lord, you have sent me to the edge of my life, so I know that you kept death from taking me out of life.

O Lord, you have sent me to the edge of my destiny, so that I know there is a second chance if I live my life doing Your holy will.

O Lord, you have sent me to the edge of my faith, so I will know that You won't put more on me than what I can bear.

My faith is in You, O Lord, and You will always know how high and how low my faith can go.

Alliance

This world has made its alliance with luck.

Many people believe in luck.

Even some church folks believe in luck to make something good happen to them.

This world has made its alliance with the unpredictable.

Many people love to be unpredictable.

They don't want to be figured out.

The Lord will always know them.

This world has made its alliance with the phenomenal.

Many people want to be extraordinary and want to do extraordinary things and not give the Lord Jesus Christ the glory and praise.

This world has made its alliance with the uncertain.

Many people are so uncertain about their lives that they don't put their trust in Jesus, who is certain to save us from our sins if we confess and repent and believe in Him.

Walk on Water Faith

Walk on water faith in the Lord is believing that Jesus will bless our spiritual gifts and make us a blessing to our church family.

Walk on water faith in the Lord is believing that Jesus Christ, our Lord, will give us the strength to overcome our weaknesses.

Walk on water faith in the Lord is believing that He will bring us through our trials.

Walk on water faith in the Lord is believing that Jesus cannot fail to be there for us when we need Him.

Walk on water faith in the Lord is beyond living by eyesight.

Many people's desires and emotions will cause them to drown in the sea of sin.

Walk on water faith in the Lord is believing that Jesus will do what He says in His holy word.

Walk on water faith in the Lord is believing that Jesus will calm the storm in our lives if we keep our eyes on Him.

Walk on water faith in the Lord is believing that Jesus is walking on the water of our hearts to surrender to Him every day.

We Can't Solve All of Our Choices

You don't know what choices I make.

I don't know what choices you will make.

We can't solve all of our choices.

I will make choices all day long.

You will make choices before you lay down to sleep.

I will make choices before I lay down to sleep.

There are big choices to make.

There are little choices to make.

We can make some big wrong choices.

We can make some little wrong choices.

We can't solve all of our choices.

You will not make all the right choices.

I will not make all the right choices.

You don't know when you will make a wrong choice.

You can make a wrong choice at any second, minute and hour.

Only the Lord can solve all of our choices.

Jesus knows all of our hearts.

Many people make choices that lead them to their death.

We don't know all the choices that we will make.

We can make a split-second choice and be wrong.

The right choices that we make are all because of God's grace.

Down in the Ocean of the Heart

Down in the ocean of the heart there are sharks of strife that love to bite with revenge.

Down in the ocean of the heart there are octopuses of malice that love to rap their legs around their prey.

Down in the ocean of the heart there are sting rays of deception that love to shock whoever crosses their path.

Down in the ocean of the heart there are whales of judgment that love to force their opinions on whoever they can swallow down in their bellies.

Down in the ocean of the heart there are crabs of gossip that love to claw whoever they can pull down in rumor.

Down in the ocean of the heart Jesus Christ, our Lord, always knows how to catch the ocean creatures of our hearts.

Jesus loves to scale the fish of motives and clean our hearts of sinning willfully against Him.

Shipwrecked

Are you shipwrecked on the island of disappointment?

Are you shipwrecked on the island of a heartache?

Are you shipwrecked on the island of fear?

Are you shipwrecked on the island of stress?

Are you shipwrecked on the island of debt?

Are you shipwrecked on the island of grief?

Are you shipwrecked on the island of trouble?

Are you shipwrecked on the island of your marriage?

Are you shipwrecked on the island of being single?

Are you shipwrecked on the island of your faith in the Lord?

We all do get shipwrecked in one way or another.

We can get shipwrecked on the island of our trials.

Paul the Apostle got shipwrecked on an island.

He was on a mission for the Lord.

The Lord always knows how to rescue us from our shipwrecks and bring us to His seashore of grace.

Plant His Garden

The Lord loves to plant His garden of love in our hearts.

We can choose or not choose to let the Lord plant His garden of love in our hearts.

The Lord loves to grow the fresh vegetables of His holy word in our hearts to give us good spiritual health.

The Lord loves to grow the fresh fruits of His spirit in our hearts so that we can be in good spiritual health.

The Lord loves to grow beautiful flowers of His grace in our hearts.

The Lord loves to plant his garden of selfless ways in our hearts so that we grow selfless.

The Lord has no pesticides of selfishness in the garden of love He plants in our hearts.

It's up to us to allow the Lord to plant His garden of salvation in our hearts.

If we confess and repent of our sins and live our lives unto the Lord Jesus Christ, he will fill our hearts with the fresh vegetables and fresh fruits of an abundant life.

His sunlight of mercy, His fresh air of forgiveness and His waters of life will nurture our hearts with spiritual things.

The Lord loves to plant his garden of joy in our hearts.

No pesticides of sorrow can destroy our hearts if we love Jesus Christ.

Around the Clock Faith

We should have an around the clock faith in Jesus Christ.

Whatever Jesus inspires us to say, we should be ready around the clock to say it.

Whatever Jesus inspires us to do, we should be ready around the clock to do it.

Jesus may wake us up out of our sleep at any late hour of the night.

We should be glad that our faith in Jesus is wide-awake for us to see how much we need Jesus in our minds and hearts.

There are many church folks who only have an hourglass faith that will run out when hard times come their way.

An around the clock faith will endure and let us keep Jesus above and beyond what is going on around the clock.

Jesus loves us and watches over us around the clock.

Jesus needs no rest and no sleep.

Jesus Knows My Heart

If I was blind, Jesus knows my heart.

If I was deaf, Jesus knows my heart.

If I was paralyzed, Jesus knows my heart.

If I couldn't say one word, Jesus knows my heart.

Many people will judge me for being blind.

Many people will judge me for being deaf.

Many people will judge me for being paralyzed.

Many people will believe that the Lord put a curse on me.

Many people will believe that I have done many terrible things.

If I don't know anything, Jesus knows my heart.

My heart is what Jesus may see to be in great spiritual health, even if my physical health looks like a curse to people who don't know my heart.

Many of the Worst Kinds of Criminals

Many of the worst kinds of criminals love to be alive.

Being alive is love.

There is no love in death, which the worst kind of criminals know about.

Even many of the worst kinds of criminals won't turn their backs on love.

Many of the worst kinds of criminals want someone to show them some love and give them some food to eat.

Many of the worst kinds of criminals want the correctional officers to show them some love and give them a jail cell they can be comfortable in.

Many of the worst kinds of criminals would want the police officers to show them some love and not kill them in a shootout.

Many of the worst kinds of criminals want the governor to show them some love and spare their lives from the death chamber.

The devil hates love.

The devil can't choose to love.

His fate is set for hell.

There is no more chance for him to love God.

The worst kinds of criminals have a chance to confess and repent of their sins and love God and their neighbors.

God's grace gives every criminal a chance to turn away from their sins.

There is no grace for the devil.

He is destined to go to hell.

God gave the devil a chance to repent, but he never did repent of his sins.

God removed his grace from the devil and his angels.

They are lost forever.

Every criminal who is still alive can choose to repent and be saved in Jesus.

If you haven't repented before you die, it will be too late for you to be saved.

God Created Eve for Adam

God created Eve for Adam to love her.

When God created Eve, she blew Adam's mind.

She was so beautiful to him.

When Eve ate the fruit that the serpent tempted her with, she gave it to Adam and he ate the fruit because he loved her so much.

God would have created another Eve for Adam if he had not eaten the fruit.

God said that it was not good for man to be alone.

We men need women in our lives.

We wouldn't be able to live in this world without women being here with us.

It's women who help us men do good in life.

It's the women who help us men wise up.

It's the women who help us men to live a long life.

It's the women who help us men have good mental and physical health.

God created a woman for the man.

This whole world would be so poisonous without women in it.

Without women in this world, we men would all die out and cease to exist.

God knew what He was doing when he created Eve for Adam.

God didn't make any mistakes, even though Eve ate the fruit and gave it to Adam.

We men cannot live without women.

And That's Just the Way It Is

Many people are brilliant and that's just the way it is.

Many people are geniuses, and that's just the way it is.

Many people are average intelligence, and that's just the way it is.

Many people are good, and that's just the way it is.

Many people are bad, and that's just the way it is.

Many people are rich, and that's just the way it is.

Many people are poor, and that's just the way it is.

Many people look good, and that's just the way it is.

Many people are smart, and that's just the way it is.

Many people are sick, and that's just the way it is.

Many people are dead, and that's just the way it is.

Many people have good common sense, and that's just the way it is.

Many people are workaholics, and that's just the way it is.

Many people are saved in Jesus, and that's just the way it is.

Many people are lost in their sins, and that's just the way it is.

Jesus Christ is the son of God, and that's just the way it is.

Jesus Christ is the light of the world, and that's just the way it is.

Jesus Christ is the way, truth, and life, and that's just the way it is.

Jesus Christ is our Lord and savior who came to this world to save us from our sins, and that's just the way it is.

Jesus Christ is coming back one day to give us eternal life, and that's just the way it is.

Can Take Away

It's the Lord who gives you beauty, and the Lord can take your beauty away if you flaunt yourself.

It's the Lord who gives you muscles, but the Lord can take away your muscles if you bully someone else.

It's the Lord who gives you intelligence, and the Lord can take away your intelligence if you think highly of yourself.

It's the Lord who gives you skills, and the Lord can take away your skills if you boast about yourself.

It's the Lord who gives you wealth, and the Lord can take away your wealth if you don't give to the poor.

It's the Lord who giveth and it's the Lord who can take it away.

The Lord has taken away things from many people who didn't give Him all the glory and praise.

It's the Lord who gives you and me life, health and strength.

The Lord can take away our life, health and strength if we don't love and obey Him.

May Never See Again

There are people who we grew up with that we'll never see again.

We hope that those people are saved in Jesus.

There are people we went to school with that we may never see again.

There are people we worked with on the job that we may never see again after they retire.

There are people we've been in the military with that we may never see again.

There are people we see in a shopping mall that we may never see again.

There are people we see at the airport that we may never see again.

There are people we see driving the roads that we may never see again.

There are people we see in church that we may never see again.

Hopefully we will one day see them in heaven where righteous people will go for being saved in Jesus Christ.

Would You Want to Become a Christian?

Would you want to become a Christian if only Jewish people were Christians?

Would you want to become a Christian if only white people were Christians?

Would you want to become a Christian if only black people were Christians?

Would you want to become a Christian if only Spanish people were Christians?

Would you want to become a Christian if only Asian people were Christians?

Would you want to become a Christian if only islander people were Christians?

Would you want to become a Christian if only Arab people were Christians?

Would you want to believe in Jesus Christ if there were only one race, creed and culture of people who believed in Jesus?

Jesus is for anyone and everyone to believe in Him and be saved.

Jesus is not just for one race, creed and color of people.

Caused by Sin

A lot of accidents are caused by not doing something right, and that comes from sin.

Murders come from sin.

Sickness comes from sin.

God is a fair God who lets everybody make their free will choices.

The wrong choices are caused by sin.

God allows our sins to make us reap what we sow.

We can't blame God for the bad things that are caused by sin.

God gave us His Son, Jesus Christ, to save us from our sins.

God will allow sin to exist until Jesus comes back again.

Many people will blame God for what sin has done and for what sin is doing.

You and I can choose to sin.

God won't stop us from choosing to sin against Him.

We can't blame God for the sins that we commit.

All bad things are caused by sin and not by God.

God doesn't make things go wrong in our lives.

Our sinful choices make things go wrong in our lives.

The devil loves to tempt us to sin.

God loves for us to pray to Him to help us to resist the devil's sinful temptations.

God doesn't tempt anyone to do evil things.

Evil things are caused by sin that comes from the devil.

What Jesus Wants

It doesn't matter what other people say. You have to say what Jesus wants you to say.

It doesn't matter what other people think. You have to say what Jesus wants you to say.

It doesn't matter how other people feel. You have to say what Jesus wants you to say.

It doesn't matter what other people think you want to do. You have to do what Jesus wants you to do.

It doesn't matter what other people do. You have to do what Jesus wants you to do.

It doesn't matter how other people feel. You have to do what Jesus wants you to do.

What truly matters is what Jesus wants — not what you and I want.

Jesus is always right about what He wants.

His holy word lets us know what Jesus wants from you and me.

We Can Want to Rush the Lord

We can want to rush the Lord to answer our prayers.

We can want to rush the Lord to bring us through our trials.

We can want to rush the Lord to bless us.

We can want to rush the Lord to work out our problems.

We can want to rush the Lord to lighten our burdens.

We can want to rush the Lord to make us well.

We can want to rush the Lord to bring more people to the church.

The Lord will never rush us to confess our sins.

The Lord will never rush us to repent of our sins.

The Lord will never rush us to love Him.

The Lord will never rush us to obey Him.

The Lord will never rush us to make our free will choices.

The Lord will never rush us to live for Him.

Even though the Lord won't rush us, if we don't deny ourselves and pick up our crosses and follow him, the devil will rush us to be lost in our sins.

The devil loves to rush us to sin against God.

Want to be Worshiped

There are people who want to be worshiped for what they say.

They believe that they can say words of all truth all the time.

There are people who want to be worshiped for what they know.

They believe that they are all-knowing and therefore know everything.

There are people who want to be worshiped for what they do.

They believe they can do all things.

There are people who want to be God, but they won't love everybody like God does.

There are people in the church who want to be God, but they can change on you and me.

The one true God will never change on us.

There are people who want to be worshiped.

They will believe they have no sins.

They will believe they are perfect in every word they say.

They will believe they are perfect in everything they do.

There are people who want to be worshiped, but they won't humble themselves unto death like Jesus Christ did to save us from our sins.

Jesus is worthy to be worshiped by angels and human beings who are not worthy to be worshiped.

Some People Believe

Some people believe that what they say must happen, just because they said it.

Some people believe that whatever they say must be true and people should believe it.

Some people will say something that's not true about someone else to make that person look bad before other people.

Some people are just bad-minded.

If they think that things may not go their way, they will say something bad about someone else to deflect blame.

They will do anything to get their way and get what they want.

Some church folks are guilty of that.

Things must go their way. If not, they will talk bad about someone else who they believe is in the way of them getting what they want.

The Pharisees talked bad about Jesus Christ, who they believed to be in the way of them keeping their power over people.

Some people believe that they must be right about whatever they say and do.

They don't care about making someone else look bad to influence people to believe that they are so holy and righteous.

You Can't Judge Someone

You can't judge someone for being of a difference race, creed or culture than you.

You can't judge someone for not being educated.

You can't judge someone if he or she disagrees with you.

You can't judge someone for not eating what you eat.

You can't judge someone for not believing what you believe.

You can't judge someone for being poor.

You can't judge someone for how he or she feels.

You can't judge someone for going through some hard times.

You can't judge someone for how he or she looks.

You can't judge someone for what he or she says.

You can't judge someone for what he or she does.

God is the judge.

You will be surprised who you see in heaven if you make it there.

Who Don't Believe

There are people who don't believe that the devil exists.

How can they not believe, when so many people are getting killed every day?

Killing is the work of the devil.

The devil is a murderer.

There are people who don't believe that sin exists.

How can they not believe, when there are many diseases and sicknesses that come from sin?

Sin is breaking God's holy law.

There are people who don't believe that there is a God.

How can they not believe, when nature is proof that there is a God?

There are people who don't believe that Jesus Christ is the Son of God.

How can they not believe, when the gospel of Jesus Christ will spread around the world?

There are people who don't believe that there is an eternal life after death.

How can they not believe, when Jesus is the resurrection to give us eternal life when he comes back again?

There are people who don't believe that there is a Holy Spirit.

How can they not believe, when it's the Holy Spirit who speaks to our consciences to let us know what is right and what is wrong?

We Can't

We can't pray on our own intelligence.

We need the Holy Spirit to make our prayers right before the Lord.

We need the Lord to help us make the right choices.

We can't make the right choices on our own.

We can't live without the Lord's approval.

We can't keep ourselves alive.

Life is from the Lord, who is beyond all the doctors and medicines.

We can't even think right on our own.

We need Jesus to be in our thoughts.

Good thinking is from the Lord.

Many people won't acknowledge that all good things come from the Lord.

We can't love and obey the Lord on our own will.

We need the Holy Spirit to help us love and obey the Lord.

Our good choices are dependent on the Lord.

The devil is all about making us make bad choices all the time.

There is nothing good in the devil.

If the Lord let him have his full way with us, we wouldn't be able to do anything good.

We Can Have No Idea

We can have no idea about some physical pain that can hit us hard.

We can have no idea about some emotional pain that can come upon us so unexpectedly.

We can have no idea about what a day will bring to us.

We can have no idea about what is ahead of us.

We can have no idea about how the Lord will bless us.

We can have no idea about how the Lord will allow us to be a blessing to someone.

We can have no idea about where the Lord will send us.

We can have no idea how far the Lord will take us in our lives.

We can have no idea about who the Lord will move out of our way for us so that we can get closer to him.

We can have no idea about what we need that the Lord can give to us, always on time.

We can have no idea when our prayers will be answered.

The Lord is never too late to answer our prayers.

Spiritual Exercise

We need to always get our spiritual exercise that won't make us tired for loving the Lord.

Praying is spiritual exercise that won't make us get tired of praying for loving the Lord.

Reading the bible is spiritual exercise that won't make us get tired of reading the bible for loving the Lord.

Using our spiritual gifts to win souls is a spiritual exercise that won't make us get tired of using our spiritual gifts for loving the Lord.

Being in church is a spiritual exercise that won't make us get tired of being in church for loving the Lord.

While physical exercise can make us get tired, spiritual exercise won't make our bodies tired at all.

Spiritual exercise won't make our minds tired, spiritual exercise will energize our minds to keep them going strong in the Lord day after day.

Living our lives unto the Lord is a spiritual exercise that we won't get tired of for loving the Lord.

We Are Not Without Sin

We are not without sin.

Sin will cause us to think a wrong thought.

We are not without sin.

Sin will cause us to make a mistake.

We are not without sin.

Sin will cause us to make a wrong choice.

We are not without sin.

Sin will cause us to say something wrong.

We are not without sin.

Sin will cause us to age and get old.

We are not without sin.

Sin will cause us to die one day.

Only Jesus Christ, our Lord and savior, is without sin.

He will save us from being lost in our sins.

We are not without sin to cast a stone at anyone else.

Jesus is without sin to cast a stone at all of us who will be stoned by death if we are not saved.

You Will Know

You will know that you have the holy ghost.

If you love Jesus, you will know that you have the holy ghost.

You will know that you have the holy ghost.

If you love your neighbors, you will know you have the holy ghost.

If you pray to Jesus Christ every day, you will know you have the holy ghost.

If you put your trust in Jesus, you will know you have the holy ghost.

If you wait on Jesus to work things out for you, you will know if you have the holy ghost.

If you are a witness of Jesus, you will know you have the holy ghost.

If you give testimonies of Jesus, you will know you have the holy ghost.

If you humble yourself unto Jesus, you will know you have the holy ghost.

If you worship Jesus, you know you have the holy ghost.

If you come together with your brothers and sisters in the household of faith, you know you have the holy ghost.

If you love and provide for your family in your own household, you will know you have the holy ghost.

If you read the bible and live by it every day, you know you have the holy ghost.

If you use your spiritual gifts for Jesus, you know you have the holy ghost.

What Matters to Jesus

It doesn't matter to Jesus if you are brilliant.
It doesn't matter to Jesus if you are smart.
It doesn't matter to Jesus if you are average intelligence.
It doesn't matter to Jesus if you are educated.
It doesn't matter to Jesus if you are rich.
It doesn't matter to Jesus if you are upper middle class.
It doesn't matter to Jesus if you are poor.
It doesn't matter to Jesus if you are skillful.
It doesn't matter to Jesus if you are talented.
It doesn't matter to Jesus if you have a beautiful house.
It doesn't matter to Jesus if you have a brand-new car.
It doesn't matter to Jesus if you have an old house.
It doesn't matter to Jesus if you have an old car.
What matters to Jesus is that you love your neighbors.
What matters to Jesus is that you live your life unto Him.
What matters to Jesus is that you are saved in Him.

Love to Receive

A lot of people love to receive but they don't love to give.

A lot of people love to receive money but they won't give anyone some money.

They won't even give someone a dollar.

A lot of people are happy to receive something good from someone, but they hate to give someone something good.

A lot of people love to receive God's blessings, but they won't give God any of their time.

A lot of people love to receive God's blessings, but they won't give God any of their talents.

A lot of people love to receive God's blessings, but they won't give God any tithes or offerings.

A lot of people love to receive God's blessings, but they won't give God their hearts.

The Lord says that it's more blessed to give than to receive.

Many People Don't Care

Many people don't care about putting their lives in danger.

They don't care to see that doing foolish things can even cause them to lose their lives.

Many people believe that doing foolish things is fun and games.

Many people will see someone do something foolish and they will be a copycat and do the same foolish thing.

Many people will do something foolish to get some attention and make themselves feel good.

Many people don't care about being wise and using good judgment in their lives.

Many people enjoy doing foolish things, like it's something good to do.

Many people don't care about talking foolishly.

They can say words that just don't make any good sense.

Many people live their lives doing foolish things.

That's all that they love to do.

Many people will get high off of putting their lives in danger.

To them, it's like getting high from smoking some marijuana.

The Lord is so merciful to people who love to do foolish things.

Many people will go over their limit and lose their lives doing too many foolish things.

Fit Into

A real, true Christian won't fit into lying to people.

A real, true Christian won't fit into looking down on people.

A real, true Christian won't fit into putting people down.

A real, true Christian will fit into telling people the truth.

A real, true Christian will fit into loving people.

A real, true Christian will fit into encouraging people.

A real, true Christian won't fit into living in adultery.

A real, true Christian won't fit into fornicating.

A real, true Christian won't fit into using people.

A real, true Christian won't fit into being prejudiced against people.

A real, true Christian will fit into helping people.

A real, true Christian will fit into being real with people.

A real, true Christian won't fit into being a friend to this world.

A real, true Christian will fit into being a friend to Jesus.

A real, true Christian won't fit into living to please this world.

A real, true Christian will fit into living to please Jesus Christ.

Will Not Accept the Truth

Many people will not accept the truth in their marriage.

Many people will not accept the truth in their job.

Many people will not accept the truth in their neighborhood.

The truth is what is going on in our lives.

Many people will not accept the truth in their relationships.

Many people will not accept the truth in their homes.

Many people will not accept the truth about themselves.

The truth is who we are.

Many people will not accept the truth in their motives.

Many people will not accept the truth in their intentions.

Many people will not accept the truth in the courtroom.

The truth will set us free from lies.

Many people will not accept the truth when they hear the truth.

Many people will not accept the truth when they see the truth.

Many people will not accept the truth in the church

The truth is Jesus Christ.

Many people will not accept the truth when they read it in the bible.

A Mystery

A mystery is something that we can't figure out

A mystery is something that we don't understand.

A mystery is something that we can't reason through.

A mystery is something that we can't solve.

A mystery is something that is strange.

A mystery is something that is puzzling.

A mystery is a trick that we don't know.

There are some people who are like a mystery.

They say some strange words and do some strange things.

A mystery is something that we can be so drawn to.

A mystery is something that is unknown to us.

Some of God's ways are strange and always good for us.

A mystery is the free will.

We don't always know what choice we will make to be a mystery.

The Lord Can Use Anyone

The Lord can use anyone to help us to wise up.

The Lord can use anyone to help us to do better.

The Lord can use anyone to help us to see the truth.

The Lord can use anyone to tell us something for our good.

The Lord can use anyone to help us to do the right thing.

The Lord can use a little child to help us to be humble.

The Lord can use a little child to slow us down.

The Lord can use a little child to motivate us.

The Lord can use anyone to help us to make the right choices.

The Lord can use anyone to give us the push that we need.

The Lord can use anyone to help us to be more aware of what we do.

The Lord can use anyone to help us to be more aware of what we say.

The Lord can use anyone to help us to hold onto Him.

The Lord can use anyone to help us to be good.

The Lord is Always on Time

The Lord is always on time to bring someone into your life to be a blessing to you.

The Lord is always on time to make you strong enough to go through what comes your way.

The Lord is always on time to get you the help that you need.

The Lord is always on time to give you another chance.

The Lord is always on time to spare your life if it's in His will.

The Lord is always on time to answer your prayers.

The Lord is always on time to bring you through your trials.

The Lord is always on time to calm the storm in your life.

The Lord is always on time to give you the encouragement you need.

The Lord is always on time to give you the push that you need.

The Lord is always on time to convict you of your sins.

The Lord is always on time to save you from your sins.

The Lord is always on time to cleanse you of your sins.

The Lord is always on time to give you his holy spirit.

The Lord is always on time to reject you if you continue to reject Him.

My Body is Your Holy Temple

My body is Your holy temple, my Lord Jesus Christ.

My body is for You to live in and for me to keep clean.

My body is for You to live in and for me to keep my breath fresh.

My body is for You to live in and for me to keep my teeth clean.

My body is not my own.

My body is not for me to eat anything that I want to eat.

My body is Your holy temple for me to eat food that is good for my body.

My body is not for me to drink anything that I want to drink.

My body is Your holy temple for me to drink what is good for my body.

My body is for You to live in and for me to take good care of.

My body is for You to live in and for me to take good care of it.

My body is not for me to dress any kind of way.

My body is not for me to expose myself.

My body is not for me to wear myself out.

My body is Your holy temple, my Lord Jesus Christ.

My body belongs to You and not to me and I should not abuse it.

The Church Will Still Go On

If the church didn't have a prison ministry, the church will still go on in Jesus' name.

If the church didn't have a men's ministry, the church will still go on in Jesus' name.

If the church didn't have a women's ministry, the church will still go on in Jesus' name.

If the church didn't have a community service, the church will still go on in Jesus' name.

The church is about coming together to worship Jesus Christ and give Him all the glory and praise.

The church is not about our ministry works that can't save us from our sins.

The church is about Jesus Christ, who can save us from our sins.

The church will always go on in Jesus' name.

The church will not go on in our name that can't save anyone from their sins.

A Lot of People

A lot of people are doing anything that they want to do.

A lot of people will say anything they want to say.

A lot of people don't care about what they say.

A lot of people don't care about what they do.

A lot of people are proud of what they say.

A lot of people are proud about what they do.

A lot of people have no shame about what they say.

A lot of people have no shame about what they do.

A lot of people see no wrong in what they say.

A lot of people see no wrong in what they do.

A lot of people don't care about how you and I feel.

A lot of people don't care about what you and I say.

A lot of people don't care about what you and I do.

A lot of people don't care about talking bad.

A lot of people doing bad things.

A lot of people don't care about you and me being Christians.

A lot of people don't care about doing the Lord's holy will.

Children

Children are to be loved.

Children love to play.

Children are not too proud to cry.

Children are good imitators.

Children are forgiving.

Children are smart.

Children are curious.

Children are humble.

Children have a good memory.

Children are little people.

Children are energetic.

Children are co-dependent.

Children are lovable.

We must be like little children to be in favor with God.

We Have to Ask

If we want to know how someone feels, we have to ask that person how they feel.

If we want to know what's on someone's mind, we have to ask that person what they're thinking.

If we want to know where someone is going, we have to ask them their destination.

If we don't hear what someone is saying, we have to ask them what they said.

If we don't see what someone else sees, we have to ask them what they saw.

Jesus Christ, our Lord and savior, wants us to ask Him for some things that we want.

Someone may not know we need help if we don't ask for it.

Asking questions proves that we don't know it all.

Jesus can answer all of our questions.

Missing Out

Many people will travel around the world like they are missing out on something.

This world has a lot of places to go.

This world has a lot of wonderful thing to marvel at.

Not everyone has the money and time to travel here and there to see the wonders of this world.

Many people will tell you and me that we are missing out on a lot of things in this world.

Many people are taking pictures and videos of places they've traveled to.

They love to show them to their family and friends.

A lot of people believe that this world is so amazing to live in.

They don't want to miss out on traveling around this world.

If we don't make it to heaven, we will truly miss out on eternal life and eternal things that are forever more advanced beyond this fallen world.

We haven't seen anything until we make it to heaven for being saved in Jesus Christ.

Jesus has so many eternal wonderful things to show to us.

The wonders of heaven will blow our minds as we travel around the heavens.

You and I can miss out on a lot of things in this world, but it's nothing compared to missing out on heaven.

For All Who are Still Alive

It is the Lord's reason for all who are still alive, it's not because of luck.

It is the Lord's reason for all who are still alive, it's not because of a mystery.

It is the Lord's reason for all who are still alive, it's not because of a phenomenon.

It is the Lord's reason for all who are still alive, it's not because of any hero.

It is the Lord's reason for all who are still alive, it's not because of any doctor.

It is the Lord's reason for all who are still alive, it's not because of any scientist.

So many people are going back to the dust of the earth.

Many good people are going back to the dust of the earth.

Many young people are going back to the dust of the earth.

Many children are going back to the dust of the earth.

Many old people are going back to the dust of the earth.

Many bad people are going back to the dust of the earth.

The Lord's reasons are not for us to always question.

The Lord's reasons are always good and right for the living and the dead.

Your Enemy

Your enemy will not talk nice to you.

Your enemy will not treat you right.

Your enemy will talk bad about you.

Your enemy will give you evil eye looks.

Your enemy will try to use you.

Your enemy will hate you.

Your enemy will tell you lies.

Your enemy will try to discourage you.

Your enemy will try to pull you down.

Your enemy will try to make you look stupid.

Your enemy will despise you.

Your enemy will not want you to be successful.

Your enemy will not like you for telling the truth.

Your enemy will not like you for believing in Jesus Christ.

Your enemy will not like you for living a Christian life.

Your enemy will try to turn you away from the Lord Jesus Christ.

Perfection

We can try to strive for perfection in what we say.

We can try to say all the right words but that won't happen all the time because we are not perfect in every word that we say.

We can try to strive for perfection in what we do.

We can try to do all the right things, but that won't happen because we are not perfect in everything that we do.

Only Jesus Christ is perfect in every word that He says.

Only Jesus Christ is perfect in everything that he does.

Jesus will never make a mistake or do something wrong.

You and I can try to publish a book.

After the book is published we may see a misspelled word that can displease us.

We can try to make the book perfect, but that may not happen and we must accept it.

We can try to strive for perfection but in order to get there we will make some mistakes and we must learn from them in order to improve on what we say and do.

Perfection doesn't come easy, it takes a lot of practice.

Only Jesus can give us the best perfection for doing His holy will.

We Christians Need To

We Christians need to stay away from places that will arouse our minds.

We Christians need to stay away from places that will seduce our eyes.

We Christians need to stay away from places that will excite our senses.

We Christians need to always pray to the Lord for wisdom.

We Christians need to always pray to the Lord for strength.

We Christians need to always pray to the Lord for guidance.

We Christians need to always trust the Lord.

We Christians need to always obey the Lord.

We Christians need to always keep our minds on the Lord.

It's so easy for the wrong things to get into our minds.

We Christians need to always keep our eyes on the Lord.

It's so easy for the wrong things to deceive our eyes.

We Christians need to always sense the presence of the Lord.

It's so easy for us to sense what makes us feel good but may not be good for us.

The presence of the Lord is felt very much in His holy word.

Many things in this world will excite our senses and cause us to not feel the presence of the Lord.

It's Not Our Time to Judge

It's not our time to judge anyone on this earth.

The Lord is still in the saving business and gives everyone a chance to be saved in Him.

It's not our time to judge people who lost their homes, businesses or lost their lives in an earthquake, tornado, hurricane or flood.

We can judge people and believe that they must be living a wicked life because they've lost everything they have.

Job in the bible was an upright man who lost everything he had.

We don't know the reason why disasters occur in certain places where there are good and bad people.

A bad thing can happen to you and me even if we're living right by the Lord.

We won't' want people to judge us and believe that we must be doing something evil because something bad happened to us.

When we get to heaven, we will be able to judge even the fallen angels who rebelled against God.

It's not our time to judge anyone right now.

Only the Lord Jesus Christ can judge.

He knows everyone's heart beyond what anyone has lost in a natural disaster.

Just because some people have lost everything they had, it doesn't mean they are evil.

It's not our time to judge in this life on earth.

Our Little Hardships

We may go through little hardships and may complain even to the Lord.

There are many people who are blind and can't see.

There are many people who can't hear.

There are many people who have no arms and no hands to hold anything.

There are many people who have no legs and no feet to walk on.

A lot of those people won't complain about the condition they are in.

It's an everyday hardship for them.

You and I may go through a little hardship and we may want to question the Lord.

We may say, "Why me?"

There are many people who can tell me and you that we are so blessed to have all of our body parts.

They can tell you and me that we are so blessed to have eyes to see.

They can tell you and me that we are so blessed to hear.

They can tell you and me that our complaints are an insult to the Lord.

Our little hardships are nothing big to many people who are dying from starvation.

Our little hardships are nothing big to many people who are dying from cancer and other terrible diseases.

Many people will tell you and me that we are so blessed to be in good mental health and in good physical health because we take care of ourselves.

Many people will go through some hardships and won't believe that they need the Lord.

The Lord's is merciful to get us through the little hardships and the big hardships.

If We Love the Lord Jesus Christ

If we love the Lord Jesus Christ, we will never run out of thoughts about the Lord.

If we love the Lord Jesus Christ, we will never run out of talking about the Lord.

If we love the Lord Jesus Christ, we will never run out of obeying the Lord.

If we love the Lord Jesus Christ, we will never run out of praying to the Lord.

If we love the Lord Jesus Christ, we will never run out of having a relationship with the Lord.

If we love the Lord Jesus Christ, we will never run out of using our gifts for the Lord.

If we love the Lord Jesus Christ, we will never run out of worshiping the Lord.

If we love the Lord Jesus Christ, we will never run out of knowing and living by His holy word.

There is no end to Jesus Christ for us to ever run out of spiritual things.

The Same Temptations

The devil will tempt us with the same temptations every day.

He knows our weaknesses to tempt us.

You and I pretty much know our weaknesses.

The Lord knows our weaknesses, and every day He gives us the strength that we need to resist the devil's temptations.

The same temptations will come our way with some new temptations from the devil.

Some of the devil's temptations can be so strong.

The Lord will not let the devil tempt us with more than we can bear.

His temptations will not overtake us.

We can choose to pray to the Lord to help us to not give into the devil's temptations.

The devil can't make us give into his temptations.

The devil loves to prey on our weaknesses with the same temptations every day.

The devil has no power over our free will choices, even if he tries to tempt us with the same temptations every day.

May Not Know Why

Some people can say some words that are not kind, and they may not know why they said them.

Some people can do some things that are not good, and they may not know why they did them.

Can we say some words that are not nice and not know why we said them?

Can we do some things that are not good and not know why we did them?

Sin can cause us to not know why we said some words that weren't kind.

Sin can cause us to not know why we did something that was not good.

We will very often know why we said something that was not kind.

We will very often know why we did something that was not good.

Many people will reject Jesus Christ and not know why they, and not care to know why.

Are Too Comfortable

A lot of people are too comfortable. They live their lives like there is nothing bad going on in this world.

A lot of people are too comfortable. They live their lives like heaven is on earth.

A lot of people are too comfortable. They live their lives like there is no devil here on earth.

A lot of people are too comfortable. They live their lives like they will live to see another day.

A lot of people are too comfortable. They live their lives like this world will fulfill their lives.

A lot of church folks are too comfortable. They live their lives like God's probation won't close on them at any day.

No one can afford to be too comfortable.

We don't know when God will remove His saving grave from this world.

Dangerous Waters of Life

Many people will swim in the dangerous waters where sharks will attack them.

Some people will survive a shark attack and some people will not live through it.

In the dangerous waters of life there are shark attacks of crimes being committed every day.

The crime sharks will have a big bite that we see on the daily news.

In the dangerous waters of life we have shark attacks of politics taking a big bite in the political arena where politicians love to argue with one another.

In the dangerous waters of life there are shark attacks of the economy taking a big bite from many people's checks, as if they haven't worked at all.

Many people are swimming in dangerous waters where the sharks will surely attack them at any time.

In the dangerous waters of life there are shark attacks in many of the churches.

There are big shark bites of people believing they are saved by grace and don't have to keep the commandments of God.

The Pharisees were like sharks, trying to attack Jesus Christ with their jealously and plots against Him.

Jesus walked on the dangerous waters and the sharks could not attack him.

What is Real

Some people don't like people who are real about what they say and what they do.

There are people who won't like you and me for being real about who we are.

Many people won't like you and me for being real about Jesus Christ.

Jesus is real in the bible that tells the truth about Him.

Many people can't handle what is real. They would rather live a fairy tale life.

Many people can't deal with what is real. They don't want to accept it because it will hurt their hearts.

A dream is like a bubble that will burst when we acknowledge what is real in this world.

What is real is Jesus saving us from our sins if we believe in Him.

What is real is life is short.

What is real is God's love for us, who are not always real with God and one another.

Talking Too Much

Talking too much can cause you and me to say something wrong.

Talking too much can cause you and me to lose friends.

Talking too much can cause you and me to be disliked.

Talking too much can cause you and me to make some enemies.

Talking too much can cause you and me to not be trusted.

Talking too much can get you and me into some trouble.

Talking too much can get you and me killed.

Talking too much can cause people to ignore us.

Talking too much can cause people to not want to hear us.

Talking too much can cause you and me to not listen to what someone has to say.

When Jesus Christ lived on earth, He never talked too much.

He told people the truth that they needed to hear.

He didn't talk too much about Himself being the living truth.

He didn't give people too much truth too soon.

Jesus knew when to talk at the right time.

Jesus is Always Fair

Jesus is always fair to let us choose what we want to eat, whether it's good food or bad food; we can choose.

Jesus is always fair to let us choose what we want to drink, whether it's a good drink or a bad drink; we can choose.

We can't blame Jesus if our health goes bad.

Jesus is always fair to let us think what we want to think, whether our thoughts are good or bad.

Jesus is always fair to let us say what we want to say, whether what we say is good or bad.

We can't blame Jesus if we think wrong or say something wrong.

Jesus is always fair to let us love who we want to love.

Jesus is always fair to let us dislike who we want to dislike.

We can't blame Jesus if we don't get any love or are disliked.

Jesus is always fair to let us do what we want to do.

We can't blame Jesus when things go wrong for us.

Jesus is always fair to let us choose to live for Him.

Jesus is always fair to let us choose to live for the devil.

We can't blame Jesus if we are lost in our sins.

Will You Still?

If you run out of money, will you still trust God?

If you get sick, will you still trust God?

If you are dying, will you still trust God?

If you lose your job, will you still trust God?

If you lose your house, will you still trust God?

If you lose your car, will you still trust God?

If you lose your spouse, will you still trust God?

If you lose your friend, will you still trust God?

If you lose your health, will you still trust God?

If you lose your business, will you still trust God?

If you lose your wealth, will you still trust God?

If you lose your children, will you still trust God?

Job lost everything he had, but Job still trusted God.

Because of this trust, God gave Job more than what he had before.

Deep

A hole in the ground can be deep.

The oceans are deep.

Our thoughts can be deep.

Our words can be deep.

Deep can be bottomless.

Deep can be depthless.

Deep can be immeasurable.

Deep is beneath.

Deep is below.

Deep is far down low.

Nothing in this world can get deeper than God's holy word.

Nothing in this world can get deeper than Jesus, whose words were too deep for the Pharisees.

The Splendor of God's Love

The splendor of God's love for us is that we can move around and go here and there.

The splendor of God's love for us is that we can reason things out in our minds.

The splendor of God's love for us is that we can choose right from wrong.

The splendor of God's love for us is that we are alive to call on Jesus' name.

The splendor of God's love for us is that we can be saved in Jesus.

The splendor of God's love for us is that we can live our lives doing His holy will.

The splendor of God's love for us is that we can love Jesus and love one another while we live.

It's Not Me It's You, O Lord

It's not me who can do anything but fail. It's You, O Lord, who can do anything but fail.

It's not me who has no sins to confess and repent of. It's You, O Lord, who has no sins.

It's not me who is all-wise. It's You, O Lord, who is all-wise.

It's not me who is all-knowing. It's You, O Lord, who is all-knowing.

It's not me who will always say the right words. It's You, O Lord, who will always say the right words.

It's not me who will always do right. It's You, O Lord, who will always do right.

It's not me who will save myself from being lost. It's You, O Lord, who can save me from being lost.

You Looked Down Through

My Lord Jesus Christ, you looked down through every generation and saw how sin has messed us up so bad.

You foresaw that you had to give up your life and die for our sins.

You looked down through all of that mess that Adam and Eve made when they disobeyed You.

You, O Lord, know that we really don't see the disaster of our sins.

We are so messed up in sin that our unseen sins will outnumber our seen sins.

My Lord Jesus Christ, You looked down through all of this world's big mess and You were willing to be the light of the world and shine your love, mercy, grace and truth in this dark, sinful world.

Every human being can be saved in You, my Lord, who looked down through every soul to save.

O what a big mess You cleaned up, my Lord, when you died on the cross and rose from the grave.

More and More

Temptations will get more and more intense in these last days.

Rebellious people will commit more and more adultery.

Rebellious people will fornicate more and more.

Rebellious people will tell more and more lies.

Rebellious people will hate God more and more.

Rebellious people will break the Sabbath more and more.

Rebellious people will kill more and more.

Rebellious people will disobey their parents more and more.

Rebellious people will use Jesus' name and make it worthless more and more.

Rebellious people will covet more and more.

Rebellious people will disobey God more and more.

Rebellious people will be more and more proud.

Rebellious people will steal more and more.

The gospel of Jesus Christ will spread more and more.

More and more people will be saved in Jesus Christ in these last days.

What Can Be Better?

What can be better than the gospel of Jesus Christ being preached throughout the world?

Science is not better. Science can't save souls like Jesus can.

What can be greater than the gospel of Jesus Christ being preached throughout the world?

Technology is not greater. Technology can't save souls like Jesus Christ can.

What can be more glorious than the gospel of Jesus Christ being preached throughout the world?

Computers are not more glorious. Computers can't save souls like Jesus can.

The gospel of Jesus Christ is more wonderful than anything in this world.

What can be more beautiful than the gospel of Jesus Christ being preached around the world?

There is No Better Truth

There is no better truth than the bible's truth.

The bible's truth will give us a full definition of this world

The bible's truth has a lot of plain and simple truths for us to know.

There is no better truth than the bible's truth, which a Christian will truly see in this world.

A Christian will very often see the truth about this world.

A Christian will very often see the truth about this world more than an unbeliever who doesn't believe in Jesus Christ.

Many people will study other books that don't have the truth of this world like the bible's truth about this world.

There is no better truth than what the bible tells us, which is the truth about God, who created this world.

No other book will tell us the truth about people like the bible.

No other book will tell us the truth about nature like the bible.

No other book will tell us the truth about God's Son, Jesus Christ, like the bible.

No other book will tell us the truth about angels like the bible.

No other book will tell us the truth about what's going on in this world like the bible's truth.

There is no better truth than the bible's truth.

We Can Take Time for Granted

We can take time for granted if we don't use the time God gives us to go to church to worship Jesus Christ.

We can take time for granted if we don't use the time God gives us to go to prayer meetings.

We can take time for granted if we don't use the time God gives us to help someone in their need.

We can take time for granted if we don't use the time God gives us to bless others with the gift that He gives to us.

We can take time for granted if we don't use the time God gives us to read the bible.

We can take time for granted if we don't use the time God gives to us to encourage someone in the Lord.

We can take time for granted if we don't use the time God gives us to go and tell someone about Jesus Christ, His only begotten Son, who never took time for granted when he lived on earth.

Heroic

If someone does something heroic, many people will put that man or woman or boy or girl on a pedestal, but it is the Lord who gives people the courage to do something heroic.

Only the Lord will never fall off his pedestal.

We all will fear something, even though there are many things that you and I won't fear in this world.

We can fear what we can't do.

Jesus feared the awful suffering he had to go through.

Jesus cried out to God, "Please take this awful suffering away from me. Yet I want your will to be done, not mine."

Jesus prayed that if it were possible, the awful hour awaiting him might pass him by.

That awful hour was death coming. His way.

No one can be more heroic than Jesus Christ, who gave up his life to save all men from their sins.

Only Jesus deserves to be put on a pedestal.

No man, woman, boy or girl can ever do what Jesus did.

Even though Jesus was afraid to die in his awful hour, he did not sin against God, who gave Him the strength to overcome His fear of the awful suffering and death.

Jesus was the most heroic man who ever lived on earth.

God Has a Purpose for Us

We exist because God has a purpose for us.

That purpose is to worship Him, love Him and obey Him.

We can get caught up in believing that we have our own purpose that didn't bring us into existence.

Many people have been deceived and believe that they can fulfill their own purpose in life.

We exist through God's purpose that was there for us before we existed in our mother's womb.

We didn't create ourselves to exist in this world, but many people believe that they are god and should be worshiped.

We can't create our own purpose in life.

That is flawed thinking and will transfer us into the grave, no matter what age we are.

God has a purpose for us through His Son, Jesus Christ, who became a sinless human being to fulfill God's purpose.

Our purpose is to keep God's ten commandments.

If we make up our own purpose in life, it's like being caught up in a tornado and not know if we will live through it.

There is a Lot More to Life

There is a lot more to life than just looking good.

Looking good can cause you to make some enemies.

There is a lot more to life than just being rich.

Being rich can cause you to not get enough sleep at night.

There is a lot more to life than just going to parties.

Going to parties can cause you to get killed.

There is a lot more to life than just getting awards.

Many men have died with their names written on awarded medals.

There is a lot more to life than just being married.

Being married has got many couples in debt.

There is a lot more to life than just traveling.

Traveling here and there has got people lost.

There is a lot more to life than just eating food.

Eating too much food has caused many people to be overweight.

There is a lot more to life than just making a good name for yourself.

Many people's good names have been ruined.

There is a lot more to life than just going to church.

Many people will go to church and have no relationship with Jesus Christ.

Will Go On and On

Time will go on and on, beyond the grave where there is no time left to give our hearts to the Lord.

Crimes will go on and on, just like we see on the daily news.

Generations will go on and on, by mothers giving birth every day.

Wars will go on and on, as words of war spread around the world.

Foolishness will go on and on, because there will always be a fool who believes and says there is no God.

Wickedness will go on and on, until this world comes to an end.

Love will go on and on because God is love, forever and ever.

Peace will go on and on, coming from God who gives you and me peace of mind when we put our trust in Him.

Life will go on and on, until Jesus Christ comes back again.

The gospel of Jesus Christ will go on and on, until Jesus is preached around the world.

Jesus Christ, our Lord and savior, will go on and on while the devil and his fallen angels will be destroyed in fire and brimstone.

It's Nothing Wrong

It's nothing wrong for a man to look at a woman who looks good.

It is wrong if he has sexual thoughts about her.

It's nothing wrong for a woman to look good.

It is wrong if she is proud about looking good and lets it go to her head.

It's nothing wrong about being rich.

It is wrong if you don't give to the poor.

It's nothing wrong about getting angry.

It is wrong if you get angry and say or do something bad.

It's nothing wrong to help people in need.

It is wrong if they try to use you for helping them.

It's nothing wrong about not seeing a mistake coming our way.

It is wrong if we see that it would be a mistake to say or do something wrong.

It's nothing wrong about us having gifts and talents.

It is wrong if we want the glory and praise that belongs to the Lord.

We are All Guilty

We are all guilty of not always trusting the Lord.

We are all guilty of not always boasting about the Lord.

We are all guilty of not always praying to the Lord.

We are all guilty of not always denying self to pick up our cross and follow the Lord.

We are all guilty of not always believing that the Lord can't fail us.

We are all guilty of not always being true to the Lord.

We are all guilty of not always confessing all of our sins unto the Lord.

We are all guilty of not always giving all of our burdens to the Lord.

We are all guilty of not always giving all the glory and praise to the Lord.

We are all guilty of not always doing everything right unto the Lord.

The Lord sees all of our guilt and covers it over with His grace and mercy.

Will Pretty Much

People will pretty much talk to who they want to talk to.

People will pretty much listen to who they want to listen to.

People will pretty much love who they want to love.

People will pretty much marry who they want to marry.

People will pretty much date who they want to date.

People will pretty much argue with who they want to argue with.

People will pretty much hate who they want to hate.

People will pretty much smile at who they want to smile at.

People will pretty much laugh at who they want to laugh at.

People will pretty much fight who they want to fight.

People will pretty much kill who they want to kill.

People will pretty much offend who they want to offend.

People will pretty much use who they want to use.

People will pretty much lie to who they want to lie to.

People will pretty much tell the truth to who they want to tell the truth to.

Church people will pretty much go to church whether they are Christians or hypocrites.

The Lord will pretty much suffer long with every body to be saved.

Christian

A bright sunlight-day Christian will brighten up our days with encouragement from the words of the Lord.

A cloudy rainy-day Christian will complain about his or her problems and not put their trust in the Lord.

A warm clear day Christian will help someone in need, and give Jesus the glory and praise.

A cold day Christian will put things above the Lord and not spend much time in prayer.

A hot day Christian will keep his or her eyes on people and not trust the Lord to deal with people.

A warm night Christian will meditate on the Lord for all that He did in his or her life.

A cold night Christian will let things worry him or her and draw away from the Lord.

A hot night Christian will not be thankful for being blessed by the Lord.

I Am Like

I am like being lost out in the ocean without You, my Lord, being on my mind.

I am like being lost in outer space without You, my Lord, being in my heart.

I am like being lost in the desert without You, my Lord, being in my words.

I am like being lost in the wilderness without You, my Lord, being in what I do.

I am like being lost on the highway without You, my Lord, being my coming and going here and there.

I am like being lost on a country road without You, my Lord, being in my decisions.

I am like being lost in the dark night without You, my Lord, being in my life.

O Lord, I Need You This Day

O Lord, I need you this day and I need You to give me strength to get through this day.

O Lord, I need you to keep me in my right mind this day that I need to think on You.

O Lord, I need you this day to keep my body in good health this day that can seem to be eternal.

If I am very sick and need to get well, this day can seem to be eternal.

If I get in an accident and need to be admitted into the hospital, this day can seem to be eternal.

If I am in great danger and need protection, O Lord, I need you this day that trouble can come my way.

O Lord, I need you this day that can't promise me life to live.

This day can seem to be eternal if I am not doing anything.

This day can seem to be eternal if I am stuck in a rut.

O Lord, I need you this day to get me through the uncertain situations that can seem to be eternal if things are moving slowly and not fast enough for me.

O Lord, I need you this day, and only You, O Lord, can promise me I'll see tomorrow.

It Doesn't Matter

It doesn't matter how rich you are. If you are living in sin, you will be lost.

It doesn't matter how brilliant you are. If you are living in sin, you will be lost.

It doesn't matter how beautiful you are. If you are living in sin, you will be lost.

It doesn't matter how handsome you are. If you are living in sin, you will be lost.

It doesn't matter how skillful you are. If you are living in sin, you will be lost.

It doesn't matter how much you go to church. If you are living in sin, you will be lost.

It doesn't matter how many faults you have.

Jesus gave up His life and rose from the grave to save you and me from our sins if we confess and repent unto Him.

Trials

Trials will come our way in big and small ways.

We don't always pass the test of faith in Jesus when some trials beat us up.

When we think that the Lord is not with us, He is closer to us than we can ever realize.

We can abandon the Lord, believing that His is not with us in our trials.

Many people don't have faith as big as a mustard seed when trials come their way.

Their faith in the Lord is small and they worry about what they can't fix.

When some people go through trials, they will take things into their own hands as if they can work them out themselves.

We don't see Jesus Christ, but He can surely work things out for us always on time.

Many church folks don't have much faith in the Lord.

They believe that they can outdo the Lord.

They put their trust in themselves to get them through their trials.

If their trials are too much for them, they fall apart instead of calling on Jesus to help them get through it.

Our trials are never too much for Jesus to crush under His feet, just like Jesus crushed the serpent's head.

Even if We Only

Even if we only say but a few words to one or two of our brothers and sisters in the church, we should pray for their souls to be saved in our Lord Jesus Christ.

Even if we don't have much to say to some people in the church, we should always love them as if we talk to them a lot.

Words don't usually come to us so easily and it's difficult to talk to everyone in a one-on-one conversation in the church and outside the church.

It's so easy to always talk to who we live with in our house.

Jesus Christ, our Lord and savior, knew what to say to everyone when he lived here on earth.

Jesus knew the heart of everyone and knew whether to say a lot of words or only a few to people.

Even if we only say a few words to a brother or a sister in church, we should never have ill feelings towards them.

Jesus talks to them when we may not say a word to them.

When You Answer My Prayers

When You answer my prayers, O Lord, it makes me feel so good in my heart.

When You answer my prayers, O Lord, it makes me feel so at peace in my mind.

When You answer my prayers, O Lord, it makes me feel so strong mentally and emotionally.

When You answer my prayers, O Lord, it makes me feel so very sure that things are so much better.

When You answer my prayers, my Lord and savior Jesus Christ, I feel so complete in my life.

When You answer my prayers, my Lord Jesus, I feel so thankful in my heart.

When You answer my prayers, my Lord Jesus, I feel so on top of this world.

When You answer my prayers, my Lord Jesus Christ, I feel so free like a bird flying in the sky.

When You answer my prayers, my Lord Jesus, I feel so spiritual, like I can walk on air.

O Lord, You Will Surely

O Lord, You will surely supply all of my needs because You surely know all of my needs.

I don't know all of my needs.

I can want some things that I don't need.

O Lord, You will surely give me what I need day after day.

My needs are a lot more important than my wants.

My wants will never out last my needs.

O Lord, You will surely bless me with my needs that I don't deserve to get from you.

My needs will outnumber my wants.

I don't see all of my needs when I can see what I want.

You, my Lord, do not slack in giving me what I need.

I can want something that I don't need.

I can give up a need for something I want.

Needs are always a sure thing from You, my Lord and savior Jesus Christ.

You may give me something that I want, to show me that I don't need it.

My needs and my wants are so different, like the day is different from the night.

O Lord, You will surely give me my needs to help me to survive, when my wants can sometimes harm me.

It's a Foolish Thing

It's a foolish thing to see trouble and walk into it.

It's a foolish thing to keep company with a criminal.

It's a foolish thing to tailgate someone who is driving the speed limit or not driving the speed limit.

It's a foolish thing to talk too much.

It's a foolish thing to be proud of yourself.

It's a foolish thing to not believe the truth.

It's a foolish thing to be opinionated about someone.

It's a foolish thing to overwork yourself.

It's a foolish thing to commit a crime.

It's a foolish thing to pray for what you don't need.

It's a foolish thing to put your life in danger if it's not for a good reason.

It's a foolish thing to not use your common sense.

It's a foolish thing to do evil things.

It's a foolish thing to not believe in Jesus Christ.

It's a foolish thing to turn your back on Jesus Christ.

When We Pray

When we pray, the sunshine of our hope will shine so bright in our lives.

When we pray, the full white moonlight of our faith will glow so majestic in our lives.

When we pray, the dark clouds of our doubt will clear up in our lives.

When we pray, the raindrops of our worries will stop falling in our lives.

When we pray, the thunder of our fears will stop roaring in our lives.

When we pray, the lightning of our troubles won't strike in our lives.

When we pray to our Lord and savior Jesus Christ, the strong words of our hearts will stop blowing and make peace in our lives.

That is Hard Reality

The color of your skin may very have something to do with how you are treated.

That is hard reality.

The color of your skin may very well have something to do with how far you will go in life.

That is hard reality.

The color of your skin may have something to do with how successful you will be in life.

That is hard reality.

The color of your skin may very well have something to do with whether you're liked or disliked.

That is hard reality.

The color of your skin may have something to do with you being looked up to or being looked down upon.

That is hard reality.

Many people don't like to face up to the hard reality that skin color influences many things in their lives.

Is it possible that back in the bible days many Jews disliked the gentiles because of the color of their skin?

We know that many Jews had the opinion that the gentiles were unclean.

Jesus Christ gave up his life for everyone, regardless of their skin color.

That is hard reality to the devil and anyone who is like the devil.

Grow on You and Me

There are some people who you and I may not like at first sight, but as time goes on those people may grow on us in some good ways.

It takes time to know people through their regular words and regular actions. This shows you and me who they really are.

There are some people who you and I like right away, while there are others that take some time to like.

That is how it is with some people who have to grow on you and me, hopefully in some good ways.

Even in the church there are some people who have to grow on you and me before we like them.

You and I must love people for our souls to be saved in Jesus Christ, but it doesn't mean that you and I will always like their ways.

Jesus loves us, but he hates our sinful ways.

It will take some time for you and me to grow on some people who may not like some of our ways.

Jesus loves us all right away and will save us from our sins.

Heart Is In

Many people's heart is in what this world can offer them.

Every Christian's heart is in what Jesus Christ can offer us.

Many people's heart is in how much money they can make.

Many people's heart is in what they can achieve in this life.

Every Christian's heart is in believing in Jesus Christ.

Many people's heart is in what they can get in life.

Many people's heart is in putting their trust in this world.

Every Christian's heart is in being saved in Jesus Christ.

Many people's heart is in being self-righteous.

Many people's heart is in abusing and killing people.

Every Christian's heart is in being cleansed of our sins in Jesus Christ.

Many people's heart is in telling lies.

Many people's heart is in living a lie.

Every Christian's heart is in letting the truth of God's holy word set us free.

Boast About Jesus Christ

Don't' boast about your house.

Boast about Jesus Christ who can put you in a heavenly mansion.

Don't boast about your vehicle.

Boast about Jesus Christ who gives you life, health and the strength to get here and there.

Don't boast about yourself.

Boast about Jesus Christ who can do anything but fail, when you and I can fail to do a small task.

Don't boast about your denominational title

Boast about Jesus Christ who can save you and me and cleanse us of our sins.

Our denominational title can't save our souls and cleanse us of our sins.

Don't boast about what you can do.

Boast about Jesus Christ who can do all things.

Don't boast about what you know.

Boast about Jesus Christ who knows all things in heaven and on earth.

Don't boast about any kind of creature.

Boast about Jesus Christ who created every creature in this world for His purpose.

Is a Prison to be Locked Up In

Strife is a prison to be locked up in.

Gossip is a prison to be locked up in.

Backbiting is a prison to be locked up in.

Pride is a prison to be locked up in.

Greed is a prison to be locked up in.

Jealousy is a prison to be locked up in.

Fornicating is a prison to be locked up in.

Adultery is a prison to be locked up in.

Lying is a prison to be locked up in.

Being a glutton is a prison to be locked up in.

Hatred is a prison to be locked up in.

Being prejudiced is a prison to be locked up in.

Being self-righteous is a prison to be locked up in.

Unnatural affection is a prison to be locked up in.

Demons are the correctional officers in the prisons of sin.

The devil is the chief warrant officer of the prison of sin.

Only Jesus Christ can set us free from the prison of sin.

We must confess and repent of our sins for Jesus Christ to set us free.

So Amazing

One day in the afternoon, I was watching a TV program. On the program was a beautiful young woman flying a plane with her feet because she was born without arms. It was so amazing to me to see that young woman making that great achievement in her life. She had a beautiful smile and she looked so happy as she talked about how she loves to encourage others to do great things.

If that young woman can be so amazing, then what about the Lord who can always do the impossible for you and me.

The Lord Jesus Christ is so amazing. He did amazing things when He lived on earth without sin in His flesh.

The Lord can use anyone to do something amazing.

We can put a limit on someone and believe that he or she doesn't have what it takes to do something amazing. We can do that by believing that we are better and smarter than someone else. We tend to look on the outward appearance of someone who is handicapped mentally or physically.

The Lord sees what that person can become, when you and I can overlook that potential.

The Lord is always amazing to let us live another day.

We have no power to keep ourselves alive if the Lord shuts the door on our lives.

The Lord has blessed that young woman to be so amazing to me, who knows that only the Lord can always do so many new and amazing things to surprise you and me.

To Become a Citizen of Heaven

Many foreigners are so happy to become a citizen of this great nation.

They are happy to put their right hands up and swear before the judge to be a good, law-abiding citizen.

They waited so patiently for that great moment when they would no longer be a foreigner.

Their lives changed forever when they become a citizen of this great nation.

They can't wait to share the good news with their family and friends who may not be citizens yet.

Every believer in Jesus Christ is a foreigner in this sinful world that is not a Christian's home to stay here.

When Jesus Christ comes back again one day, He will make us citizens of heaven.

We will be so happy to become citizens of heaven.

Our joy will be beyond this world.

We won't have to be sworn-in to become a citizen of heaven.

We will enter into heaven for being saved in Jesus Christ, our Lord and savior.

This great nation has some disappointments, sorrows and downfalls, regardless of being a citizen.

Heaven is a perfect place to become a citizen of.

There is no sin in heaven.

This great nation has sins to repent of unto God.

To become a citizen of heaven is to love and obey the Lord in this life during our time here on earth in this great nation where a foreigner can lose his citizenship for committing a terrible crime.

Very Often Cautious

We are very often cautious of someone of another race, creed or color.

We can have a hard time embracing them if we don't trust them.

Very often you and I can enter into a store where someone will be very cautious of us if we look different or aren't to their liking.

That person may feel threatened by the color of our skin because he or she believes that you and I are evil.

Very often many people are not very cautious of people in their own race, creed, or color because they look like them and have the same skin color.

We are so programmed to not be very cautious of people who look like us.

Many people of the world are often cautious of church folks because many church folks are not living by what they preach and teach about Jesus Christ.

Often, we need to be very cautious about ourselves and examine our motives, which Jesus will judge by his ten commandments.

Death can come our way in so many different ways that we are not very cautious of when people believe that they are safe from harm and do not need God's protection.

God is All

Science is not all truth.
God is all truth.
Technology is not all-knowing.
God is all-knowing.
Religion is not all pure.
God is all pure.
Good health is not all life.
God is all life.
Luck is not all-merciful.
God is all-merciful.
Chance is not all sure.
God is all sure.
Care is not all love.
God is all love.
Time is not all healing.
God is all healing.
A woman is not all beauty.
God is all beauty.
A man is not all strong.
God is all strong.

The president is not all powerful.

God is all-powerful.

Logic is not all right.

God is all right.

Feelings are not all real.

God is all real.

This world is not all fair.

God is all fair.

Destiny is not all over in death.

God is all God to destine us to immortality in his Son, Jesus Christ, who rose from the grave.

Jesus Was a Sinless Man of Action

Jesus not only talked about His heavenly Father, He obeyed His heavenly Father by doing His Father's holy will.

Jesus was a sinless man of action.

Jesus not only talked about healing the sick and feeding the hungry, He healed many sick people and fed many hungry people.

Jesus was a sinless man of action.

Jesus not only talked about casting out demons and raised the dead, He cast demons out of many people and raised a few dead people.

Jesus was a sinless man of action.

Jesus not only talked about giving up His life on the cross for our sins, He gave up His life for our sins.

Jesus was a sinless man of action.

Jesus not only talked about rising up from the grave, he rose from the grave.

Jesus was a sinless man of action.

Jesus talked about going back to heaven, and He went back to heaven.

Jesus was a sinless man of action.

Jesus not only talked about saving souls from their sins, He actually saves us from our sins when we confess and repent and are baptized in His holy name.

Jesus is without sin and always does what He says He will in His holy word.

Can Be Told

A lie can be told in a brilliant way.

The truth can be told in a simple way.

A lie can be told in a loving way.

The truth can be told in a hateful way.

A lie can be told in a good way.

The truth can be told in a hurtful way.

A lie can be told in a charming way.

The truth can be told in an ugly way.

A lie can be told in an attractive way.

The truth can be told in a pitiful way.

A lie can be told in a proud way.

The truth can be told in a despising way.

Jesus Christ always told the truth in love.

Many church folks won't speak the truth in love.

Many people can tell a lie in a cheerful way.

A Candle's Light to Shine

My Lord and savior Jesus Christ gave me a candle's light to shine in my life so I can do His holy will.

From my childhood to today, You extended my days for me to see this day and shine my candle's light giving You all the glory and praise.

You, my Lord, have given me a candle's light to shine in my life, giving a testimony about You bringing me out of darkness.

You gave me a candle's light to shine in my life with the spiritual gifts that You gave to me to uplift and magnify Your holy and precious name.

O Lord, You gave me a candle's light to shine in my life as I hold onto You and go through my trials.

O Lord, you gave me a candle's light to shine in my life and light this dark world that can't blow out my candle's light.

You cover Your hands over my life so the winds of darkness cannot blow it out.

Sooner or Later

If you and I tell the truth, sooner or later it will come back to us.

If you and I tell a lie, sooner or later it will come back to us.

Whatever you and I say, sooner or later it will come back to us.

Whatever you and I do, sooner or later it will come back to us.

We can often fool one another, but we can never fool the Lord.

He knows what we will say before we say it.

He knows what we will do before we do it.

We can say something that we didn't plan to say.

We can do something we didn't plan to do.

Sooner or later, whatever we say and do will come back to us.

It will come back to us in our minds and it will come back to us in our bodies.

Sooner or later the Lord will let things come back to us and sometimes it's right away.

The Mind

The mind can remember things.

The mind can forget things.

The mind can plan things.

The mind can reason.

The mind can think.

The mind can scheme.

The mind can learn.

The mind can be good.

The mind can be evil.

The mind can choose.

The mind can be intelligent.

The mind can be foolish.

The mind can be wise.

The mind that is stayed on Jesus Christ will have peace this world won't understand.

Looking Down on Us

The Lord is looking down on us from heaven.

The Lord sees our tears.

The Lord hears our cries.

The Lord sees our trials.

The Lord feels our heartaches.

The Lord feels our disappointment.

The Lord feels our grief.

The Lord is looking down on us from heaven.

The Lord Jesus Christ is coming back one day to take us to heaven with Him.

The Lord will relieve us of all our pain as if we never felt any pain at all.

The Lord is coming back for His children all over this world.

The Lord is coming back to raise all of his children from the grave.

The Lord is looking down on us from heaven.

He will give all of His children eternal life one day.

There Are People Who

There are people who don't like to talk about mental illness.

They believe people in that condition are weak-minded.

There are people who don't like to talk about their failures.

They love to cover up their failures to look like they have always been well put together.

There are people who love to be great in other people's eyes.

They love to get a lot of attention to feel good about themselves.

There are people who don't like to say no.

They love to help people, even when people don't ask them for help.

There are people who don't like to say, "Yes, I can help you."

There are people who will waste their lives away.

They just don't want to do anything to help themselves do better.

There are people who love to do too much.

They are so busy all the time that they don't have any time to sleep.

Even though there are people who don't believe in Jesus Christ, they can't stop you and me from being saved in Jesus, who we believe in.

We All Have

We all have done some things that were not good.

We don't like to talk about those bad things we did.

It makes us feel ashamed and bad.

We know that some of those things are things we just can't talk about to anyone but the Lord.

Many people have moved on beyond the bad things they did.

Many people are still holding onto those bad things they did.

We know that if we were to tell some people about the bad things we did, they would look at us in a bad way and wouldn't want to be near us.

Those bad things need to be left in the past, as long as we have changed for the better to not do those bad things anymore.

Some people, even in the church, love to remind us of those bad things we did.

They can say in direct words, pointing to you and me and saying what we did was bad.

Jesus Christ, our Lord, will wipe away those bad things if we confess and repent of our sins unto Him.

We all have done some bad things that Jesus Christ will forgive us for.

A Spiritual Warming

There is a spiritual warming for many people who have a heat wave of confessing and repenting of their sins unto the Lord Jesus Christ.

There is surely a spiritual warming for many people to get baptized and live a renewed life unto Jesus Christ.

Global warming will surely have its heat wave covering over the dry land.

Global warming will surely cause many people to get heat exhaustion.

The spiritual warming will not cause you and me to get a heat exhaustion of being born again in the spirit.

Global warming is caused by air pollution wearing out the ozone layer up in the sky.

The spiritual warming is caused by the Lord moving hearts to repent.

Global warming is caused by greed and wanting to make millions and billions of dollars.

Spiritual warming is caused by the love of Jesus, who wants to save as many souls as He can.

The Spiritual Family

If you are getting baptized, you are welcomed into the spiritual family.

You will have more brothers and sisters than you ever had before in your life.

You are now a new creature in your spiritual life.

You have joined an army of spiritual soldiers who are fighting against sinful words and sinful deeds.

In our spiritual family we have a heavenly Father who gave us His only Son to save us from our sins.

His name is Jesus Christ and he holds our spiritual family together every day.

This spiritual family is the largest family you and I can ever be in.

We have so many brothers and sisters who we can relate to about our Lord and savior Jesus Christ.

If you are getting baptized, you are entering into the best family you can ever have.

The spiritual family will stay together in Jesus' holy name.

The spiritual family is the greatest family on earth.

God Chooses All

God chooses all to be saved.

God chooses all to have a free will to choose to do good or evil.

Even though God had hardened King Pharaoh's heart, God did it so that His power and glory would be revealed to save His people and free His people from slavery.

Even though God hardened King Pharaoh's heart, it didn't mean that the king didn't have free will to choose who he would serve.

He chose to serve idol gods and not the true, living God.

God created Lucifer to worship him.

God created him perfect in all of his ways.

God didn't choose Lucifer to sin against Him.

God foresaw that King Pharaoh would not want to free His children, so God used that for His purpose to be fulfilled.

God chooses all to be saved.

Everybody will not choose to love and obey God.

The Greatest Experience

I have to experience what you experience to know how you feel.

You have to experience what I experience to know how I feel.

If I am not going through what you are going through, I don't know how you feel.

If you are not going through what I am going through, then you don't know how I feel.

I can't have an opinion about you for what you experience and you can't have an opinion about me because of what I experience.

If I have experienced what you have, then I will know how you feel.

If you have experienced what I have, then you will know how I feel.

You can tell me what you have experienced, but I don't know your experience first-hand.

The greatest experience you and I can ever have is to be born again in the newness of Jesus Christ.

WE all can go through the greatest experience of our lives for believing in Jesus Christ and living right in His spirit.

We all will know how we truly feel for loving and obeying Jesus Christ every day.

What is This World Coming To?

What is this world coming to?

There are more and more murders.

There is more and more violence.

There are more and more thieves.

What is this world coming to?

There are more and more rapists.

There is more and more sexual immorality.

There are more and more liars.

There is more and more greed.

There is more and more poverty.

There are more and more gossipers.

What is this world coming to?

There are more and more revengeful people.

There are more and more judgmental people.

What is this world coming to?

There are more and more people turning their backs on Jesus Christ.

There are more and more wolves in sheep's clothing.

There are more and more people who are lost in their sins.

Life Can

We can make plans in our lives.

Life can throw us a fast curve ball for us to get a strike.

We want our loved ones to live a very long life.

Life can cause us to fall in a deep hole of grief if our loved ones die at a young age.

We can want the best for even good people we don't know.

Life can strike us out with disappointment.

We can love people like we want to be loved.

Life can fumble us to fall into the hands of our enemies.

We can encourage people and help people.

Life can cause us to go out of bounds if we let people use us for helping them.

We can tell people about what the Lord brought us through.

Life can ball up its fist and hit us hard with people who will hold our sins against us.

We can live a renewed life in Jesus Christ.

Life can spill over its temptations on us if we don't stay in prayer.

We can be saved in Jesus Christ.

Life can videotape our comings and goings to try to prove that we are not saved.

We can have the holy ghost.

Life can cause people to look at our past sins, looking like a ghost to them that they feared.

Life can turn against us.

It doesn't matter to life if we are Christians.

Jesus can give us joy no matter what life does to us.

Commercials

Almost every TV commercial is about selling a product.

The product will pretty much get sold.

Many people will buy the products.

There are more TV commercials than TV shows.

Many people will create their products and will try their best to sell it.

They want to sell as many as they can.

They want to hopefully get rich from selling their products.

Commercials are pretty much about making lots of money off of other people.

The TV producers will show commercial after commercial because many people want their product to be seen and to be sold to the TV viewers.

They will pay a lot of money to get their commercial shown for their product to be sold.

Jesus Christ, our Lord, bought us with a price when many people will give their souls to sin for free.

Sin sees our souls and will try to rob us of the price that Jesus paid for us to be saved in Him.

Sin will only pay for its commercials to sell us its product of being lost in hell.

Human Beings are Human Beings

Human beings are human beings no matter whether they're male or female.

Human beings are human beings no matter the color of their skin.

Human beings are human beings no matter if they're normal or handicapped.

Human beings are human beings no matter if they're rich, upper middle, middle class or poor.

Human beings are human beings no matter if they're tall, short, big or small.

Human beings are human beings no matter if they're smart or dumb.

Human beings didn't come from any animal.

Human beings were created in the image of God.

The saved human beings will be made like the angels when Jesus Christ comes back again.

Jesus Christ was a human being and the Son of God.

Human beings are human beings no matter if they're good or evil.

Human beings are human beings who all have free will.

I Am Going to Make It

I am going to make it because of You, my Lord Jesus.

I need you here on earth and I will need you in heaven.

Hopefully I will make it to heaven.

I am going to make it because of You, my Lord Jesus, who will give me the strength to get through the day.

I am going to make it because of You, my Lord Jesus, who will always be there for me when I need You.

I am going to make it because of You, my Lord Jesus, encouraging me to hold onto You.

I am going to make it because of You, my Lord Jesus motivating me to start my day off with You on my mind.

I am going to make it because of You, my Lord Jesus loving me as if I was the only person here on earth.

I am going to make it because of You, my Lord Jesus leading me and guiding me to love and obey You every day.

First Impressions

First impressions about people are not always true.

You and I may see someone for the first time and we may really like that person.

You and I may see someone for the first time and we may not like that person.

The person who we may really like the first time we meet them may end up being disliked.

The person we didn't like at first may end up being liked.

It takes time to get to know someone who we may like or not like the very first time we see him or her.

Some people can really put on a good act to try to get people to like them.

Some people may be going through something really bad that causes them to be disliked by because of their appearance.

First impressions are not always true to believe.

People can change for the better or they can change for the worse.

Most church folks will change for the better because of growing stronger in the Lord.

Jesus Christ, our Lord, loves us all whether we are liked or disliked by other people at first sight.

We Christians must look beyond our first impressions to love people like Jesus loves us.

The Door on Our Hearts

One day in the afternoon, I was in my house taking care of my two little dogs.

I was in the kitchen when I looked out the window and saw my next-door neighbor.

I saw him and a lady walking on the sidewalk in front of my townhouse.

He then came to my front door and turned the doorknob to enter my house.

He thought he was at his front door.

The lady said to him, "You are at the wrong house."

I said, "Thank you, Jesus, for letting me know to keep my door locked at all times."

I felt so relieved that my front door was locked as I heard him turn the doorknob and couldn't come into my house.

I had let my dogs out in the back yard.

If they had been in the house, they would have barked to let him know that he was at the wrong house.

We can choose to lock the door on our hearts against living in sin.

We can choose to unlock the door on our hearts and let Jesus into the house of our hearts.

If we let Jesus into our hearts, we'll never regret it.

The Spiritual Ground

Children love to play on the ground.

Many people love campgrounds.

We all love to walk on the ground.

Many people love to run on the ground.

Many people love to have a cookout on the ground.

Many people love the fairgrounds.

Many people will rake the leaves up on the ground.

Many people will cut the grass on the ground.

Many people will dig a hole in the ground.

Many people will build houses on the ground.

There are so many things that we can do on the ground.

The ground is very often stable to walk on.

The ground is very often stable to live on day after day.

We will seldom get an earthquake to shake up the ground and break up the ground.

The ground will hold us all up on our feet.

There is a spiritual ground that we can spiritually walk on every day.

The spiritual ground is stable all over this world for anyone to walk on and be saved in Jesus Christ.

The spiritual ground is filled with spiritual things that are eternal.

The physical ground is filled with temporary things.

The spiritual ground is holy. And we can walk on it to go to Jesus.

The Hard Way

We will learn things the hard way if we don't listen to wise advice.

Many people will learn things the hard way by doing what they want to do even though it's wrong.

Many people are suffering right now for learning things the hard way.

They don't want to wise up and do what the Lord says.

Many people have made their own lives hard by only thinking about themselves and not caring about anyone else.

Learning things the hard way can bring on much pain and misery.

We will learn things the hard way if we don't love and obey Jesus Christ, who will not bring any hardship upon us.

You and I can give someone some wise advice, but it's wise people who will do what the Lord says in His holy word.

Learning things the hard way can make us spiritually ill and physically ill.

We church folks will learn some things the hard way if we don't take heed of God's holy word.

Will We Pass God's Test?

Will we pass God's test when the devil accuses us of not having enough faith in Jesus Christ?

Will we pass God's test when the devil accuses us of not obeying the Lord day after day?

Will we pass God's test when the devil accuses us of doing our own will?

Will we pass God's test when the devil accuses us of not trusting Jesus to work out our problems?

Will we pass God's test when the devil accuses us of not loving everyone the same?

Will we pass God's test when the devil accuses us of not having a relationship with Jesus Christ?

Will we pass God's test when the devil accuses us of not studying God's holy word?

God will allow the devil to make his accusations against us to prove to the devil that we are faithful to Jesus no matter what we go through.

Will we pass God's test when the devil accuses us of not being humble before God and one another?

Will we pass God's test when the devil accuses us of not being in church on time?

Will we pass God's test when the devil accuses us of not making our body to be God's holy temple?

Will we pass God's test when the devil accuses us of not forgiving one another?

A Story to Tell

We all have a story to tell.

Our story may not be like the story of Joseph.

We all have a story to tell.

Our story may not be like the story of Moses.

We all have a story to tell.

Our story may not be like the story of King David.

We all have a story to tell.

Our story may not be like the story of Elijah.

We all have a story to tell.

Our story may not be like the story of Esther.

We all have a story to tell.

Our story may not be like the story of Isaiah.

We all have a story to tell.

Our story may not be like the story of Jeremiah.

We all have a story to tell.

Our story may not be like the story of Hosea.

We all have a story to tell.

Our story may not be like the story of Jonah.

We all have a story to tell.

Our story may not be like the story of Apostle Paul.

We all have a story to tell.

Our story may not be like the story of Jesus Christ.

We all have a story to tell in this world, whether it's a good story or a bad story.

Reach

We must reach down low to love one another before we can reach up high to love Jesus Christ.

We must reach down low to know our own hearts before we can reach up high to know Jesus Christ.

We must reach down low to relate to one another before we can reach up high to relate to Jesus Christ.

We must reach down low to deny self before we can reach up high to be born again in Jesus Christ.

We must reach down low to humble ourselves before we can reach up high to represent Jesus Christ.

We must reach down low to wise up before we can reach up high to live right unto Jesus Christ.

We must reach down low to choose what is good before we can reach up high to choose to follow Jesus Christ who is good all the time.

We must reach down low to help those who are less fortunate than we are before we can get Jesus to shine his favor upon us.

We Shouldn't Complain

If we have a house to live in, we shouldn't complain because many people are homeless.

If we have a car to drive, we shouldn't complain because many people don't have a car to drive.

If we have a job, we shouldn't complain because many people don't have a job.

If we have an income, we shouldn't complain because many people don't have an income.

If we can pay our bills, we shouldn't complain because many people can't pay their bills.

If we have food to eat, we shouldn't complain because many people are starving.

If we have clean water to drink, we shouldn't complain because many people are drinking polluted water.

If we are educated, we shouldn't complain because many people can't read and write.

If we are going through some trials for Jesus' name's sake, we shouldn't complain because many people just don't know that Jesus can do anything but fail us.

Other Worlds

I had a dream of other worlds, even though I didn't see any life on those worlds.

Those worlds were so beautiful to look at in my dreams.

Those worlds had oceans and oceans of water.

Those worlds had beautiful buildings of towering heights.

Those worlds had glittering lights and beautiful houses everywhere.

Those other worlds were immeasurable in height, width and depth.

I was there in those other worlds in my dreams and it was so real and felt so good to me.

So far, no other has discovered any life forms on other planets in the universe.

In the book of Job, there were representatives from various planets.

They met with God on a regular basis.

Only God knows where those other worlds are in the universe.

Those other worlds could be billions of miles away from this planet.

There are other worlds in the universe.

The bible tells us so.

Spiritually Insane

Can we be spiritually insane for believing what we say about someone is true when it may not be true?

Can we be spiritually insane for believing the things in this world will fulfill us?

Can we be spiritually insane if we believe that we are doing Jesus a favor by going to church?

Can we be spiritually insane if we believe that our works will entitle us to heaven?

Can we be spiritually insane for taking Jesus lightly, like he can't work out things for us?

Can we be spiritually insane if we turn our backs on Jesus and believe that we won't regret it.

Can we be spiritually insane if we believe that we can persuade Jesus to overlook our wrongs.

This World Can't Put an End To

This world can't put an end to injustice.

This world can't put an end to prejudice.

This world can't put an end to crimes.

This world can't put an end to greed.

This world can't put an end to discrimination.

This world can't put an end to violence.

This world can't put an end to sexual immorality.

This world can't put an end to poverty.

This world can't put an end to grief.

This world can't put an end to war.

This world can't put an end to diseases.

This world can't put an end to natural disasters.

This world can't put an end to pride.

This world can't put an end to jealousy.

This world can't put an end to sickness.

This world can't put an end to heartache.

This world can't put an end to sin.

This world can't put an end to death.

Jesus Christ will put an end to all the world's defects when He comes back again.

My Life is a Lot Better

My life is a lot better because of my Lord and savior Jesus Christ, who has renewed my life for me to live right in His holy name.

My life is a lot better.

I think a lot better.

I talk a lot better.

I walk a lot better.

I act a lot better.

I eat a lot better.

I drink a lot better.

I sleep a lot better.

I dream a lot better.

I smile a lot better.

I love a lot better.

My life is a lot better.

My mind is a lot better.

My heart is a lot better.

My life is a lot better because of Jesus Christ, who can make anyone's life a lot better.

There is always room for improvement in Jesus Christ, who can make you and me right with God.

His righteousness is perfect.

I reason a lot better.

My conscious is a lot better.

I life is a lot better.

Because of Jesus my health is a lot better.

We May Feel Like

We may feel like we are stuck in a chimney, if things are not going the way we want things to go.

We may feel like we are stuck between two walls, if things are not going fast enough for us.

We may feel like we are caught up in a rip current, if we are not getting the answers we need.

We may feel like we are paralyzed, if we are not getting anywhere.

We may feel like we got beat up, if we are frustrated by a problem.

We may feel like we have been run over by a truck, if we are stressed out.

We may feel like we got blown away by a tornado, if we are grieving.

We may feel like Jesus Christ doesn't hear our prayers, if we keep praying over and over again with the same prayer.

Highway

Education is a highway to prosperity.

Laziness is a highway to poverty.

Love is a highway to relationships.

Healthy food and exercise is a highway to good health.

Beauty is a highway to drawing attention.

Sickness is a highway to death.

Selfishness is a highway to rebellion.

Protest is a highway to riot.

Strife is a highway to violence.

Wisdom is a highway to wealth.

Knowledge is a highway to power.

The mind is a highway to reasoning.

The heart is a highway to feelings.

Jesus Christ is the highway to everlasting truth and everlasting life.

www.ingramcontent.com/pod-product-compliance
Lightning Source LLC
Chambersburg PA
CBHW052140110526
44591CB00012B/1803